The Voice *of the* Rising Generation

The Voice *of the* Rising Generation

Family Wealth and Wisdom

JAMES E. HUGHES JR.
SUSAN E. MASSENZIO
KEITH WHITAKER

WILEY | **Bloomberg** PRESS

Library of Congress Cataloging-in-Publication Data:

ISBN 978-1-118-93651-1 (Hardcover)
ISBN 978-1-118-93653-5 (ePDF)
ISBN 978-1-118-93652-8 (ePub)

Printed in the United States of America

10 9 8 7 6 5 4 3 2 1

To my Rising Generation: Ellen, John, Natalie, Matt, Will, Alyssa, Ned, Catherine, Nancy-Elizabeth, and Chris; to the Next: Meg, Linnea, Sydney, Merrill, Miles, Ford, Jack, Thomas, Will, and Nadia; and to Jacqueline Merrill, who put her arm through mine.

—Jay Hughes

To Jonathan, John, Christopher, David, and Matthew—may you live lives full of health, happiness, and love.

—Susan Massenzio

To Kate, Dylan, Mary, Charli, Luke, Matt, Tristan, Cole, and Julia—may your journeys be "full of adventure, full of learning."

—Keith Whitaker

To Anne D'Andrea, the fourth author of this book: Without your support of our collaboration, this book would never have arisen. Thank you.

—From all of us

Grow up, then, my Telemachus, grow strong. . . .
Your dreams, my Telemachus, are blameless.

"Odysseus to Telemachus"
—Joseph Brodsky

Contents

Preface

B efore you set out on a journey, it is always a good idea to have some idea of where you have come from and where you are going.

We three authors come from sharing the joy of writing a previous book, *The Cycle of the Gift: Family Wealth and Wisdom* (Bloomberg, 2013). That book was directed primarily to givers within families with wealth, inviting them to a process of self-reflection and self-understanding. One of its clearest messages was that all of us within the world of family wealth—wealth creators, spouses, siblings, and advisers—need to attend much more closely to the recipients of these gifts, to their dreams, their development, and their resilience.

The reception of *The Cycle of the Gift* only added to the pleasure we felt in writing it. One participant in a meeting we convened in New England expressed what we had hoped would come from that book better than we ever could: "I received a copy of it as a gift from my adviser," he said. "I read it, and I immediately gave a copy to my mother." He went on: "Once she had read it, she sent copies to my three siblings. Reading it prompted a wonderful family meeting, such as we had never had before." Besides gratifying our all-too-human authorial egos, this response showed the cycle of the gift in action. It captured our dream that our book would bring families together to give and receive true gifts of spirit and not just transfers.

Still, while emphasizing the need to understand recipients, *The Cycle of the Gift* was addressed primarily to givers, parents, and grandparents. In it, we speak *about* recipients, generally younger members of families, but we do not truly speak *to* or *with* those younger family members. The present book aims to take that next step.

What holds these two books together is their shared focus on the core concept of *human capital*. This is a focus heralded in Jay Hughes's *Family Wealth* (Bloomberg, 2004 [1997]), as far back as its first edition, which was published two decades ago. It is a simple point, but, like most simple points, it bears repeating. Family after family whom we know focus their efforts, attention, and communications on only one of the five sources of capital available to them—their financial capital. Their human capital, which is itself the foundation of their intellectual, social, and spiritual capitals, largely goes neglected. And yet if we know anything in the field of family wealth, we know that the neglect of human capital is the ultimate cause of the dissipation of financial capital and the dissolution of families. Conversely, the cultivation of human capital strengthens family bonds and supports the preservation and growth of financial capital (not to mention intellectual, social, and spiritual capital). *The Cycle of the Gift* and *The Voice of the Rising Generation* explore and implement these basic truths. We hope that their ideas and practices benefit your family as much as they have benefited the many families from whom we have learned so much.

Acknowledgments

As authors, we would like to acknowledge our colleagues, clients, friends, and family members with whom we have discussed the challenges of the rising generation and from whom we have learned so much. Also, we would like to give special acknowledgment to Reta Haynes, the Haynes Family Foundation, and the Hemera Foundation for their generous support of our research and writing. Any insights found herein are the shared bounty of our friends; any infelicities are our own.

Introduction

A Well-Known Family

There once was a young man with a very successful father. His father came from a prominent family, but by his own industry and wits he, the father, had risen to become one of the most famous leaders of his time.

As a result, the young man, his son, grew up revering his father's name but not really knowing him as a person. As he became a young adult, he felt unsure of himself. He doubted whether he could ever accomplish much in the world, especially when compared with his father.

Luckily for this family, the young man's mother—who endured years of loneliness, far from her ambitious husband—remained a rock of constancy. And both the son and the father undertook long personal journeys to overcome their distance from each other. After many toils, the father returned home and repaired his marriage. The son underwent his own struggles, and when he at last reunited with his father, he did so both as a son and as a man of his own.

This is not the story of one of the many families with whom we have worked over the years—though, with a few changes here and there, it could apply to quite a few of them. It is the story of *The Odyssey*, the epic poem composed by Homer almost 3,000 years ago. *The Odyssey* recounts the wanderings of the hero Odysseus as he struggles to return home to the island of Ithaca from the battlefield of Troy. It also tells of the struggles of Odysseus's son Telemachus, who leaves home and goes on a quest to find his father and himself. All along, Penelope, Odysseus's wife and Telemachus's mother, endures a siege of unwelcome suitors, hoping against hope for the return of her husband and son.

The Challenge

Though Odysseus is a king and his family possesses great resources, *The Odyssey* is not primarily a story about wealth. It is a story of the human condition, and as such it speaks directly to the challenges faced by families with wealth and without it. It speaks especially to the challenge of the *rising generation*.

After years of consulting and research, we believe that we have some insight into the central challenge facing families with wealth. It is not a matter of finance. It is not a legal problem. It is not something to be resolved through the application of more, better, or faster resources. It is a human challenge, *the challenge of overcoming the silence and finding the voice of the family's rising generation*.

We will have much more to say about what we mean by "silence" and "the rising generation." But, in the spirit of giving voice to the rising generation, we would like to begin by sharing words that we have heard from young family members themselves, in talks we have given to groups of families or in family meetings we have facilitated, words similar to these:

- "I'm grateful for all my parents have done, but I sometimes feel that everything is done for me. I don't really have a voice. How can I find my own way and grow to be a happy, independent, man (or woman) of my own?"
- "I've started on my own path, but I also find myself being pulled back home through all sorts of financial or business arrangements. What are ways to keep to my own course and still remain connected with my parents and larger family?"
- "Everyone tells me to pursue my dreams. But I'm not sure what those are. I also don't know how to ask my parents about what resources I can draw on to figure out my way. Where do I start?"

Sometimes these words are very difficult for members of the rising generation to utter. At least these particular examples were spoken. In many families, in contrast, we find a deafening silence. The unspoken words of the rising generation are like Eduard Munch's *The Scream*: in our faces yet unheard.

Sometimes people think that the challenge of fostering the voice of the rising generation belongs solely to parents. Or it may be tempting to think that it lies squarely on the shoulders of members of the rising generation themselves. But this challenge does not belong just to parents or just to children. *The Odyssey* is not a story just of Odysseus's return home, nor is it a tale just of Telemachus's struggles to leave home. The rising generation needs those who have risen, and the risen need the rising.

The Journey

The goal of this book is simple: to engage in a conversation primarily with members of the rising generation, a conversation aimed at helping you meet this central challenge of growing and not losing your voice. Here is our plan:

Chapter 1 will squarely confront the main obstacle to the rising generation's finding its voice. The obstacle is, paradoxically, the great dream of the founder, which often turns into a *black hole*. In too many cases, this black hole absorbs the dreams of the individuals who came after the founder, leaving them at best to use their lives to steward somebody else's dream. This path diminishes the self, silences the future, and ultimately saps the family's vitality. It is the true cause of dependency, entitlement, and the power of the proverb "shirtsleeves to shirtsleeves (or rice paddy to rice paddy) in three generations."

With this obstacle in mind, Chapter 2 discusses what we mean by a *rising generation*. Our goal is to help you, members of the rising generation, recognize yourselves, apart from the distorting influence of the black hole. We will discuss the characteristics of members of any rising generation. We will explore the need for members of the rising generation to explore or struggle in order to grow. And we will touch upon the general challenges that members of rising generations face, with or without wealth.

Chapter 3 moves the conversation from the challenges that members of the rising generation face to strategies for dealing with those challenges. It will offer ways that you, members of rising generations, can come to know yourselves better, in particular your strengths, your beliefs, and your internal hurdles. We also share an updated version of our "Individual & Family Balance Sheet" as a tool for charting progress in this journey of self-understanding.

Chapter 4 takes the step from gaining self-knowledge to developing resilience and independence. Many parents focus primarily on financial literacy as a necessary skill for members of the rising generation. We ask young family members to reflect on what you think that you will need most to find your voice. Following Freud's emphasis on the importance of love and labor, we dwell in particular on the experience of work, managing relationships, and communicating as crucial for developing resilience, confidence, and competence within the context of family wealth.

The first four chapters lay out challenges faced by or strategies open to all members of rising generations in families with wealth. In Chapter 5, we apply this learning to the specific challenges faced by family members in the *middle passage* of life. If you are in this situation, you may have lived with decades of silence but now want to find your voice. We discuss ways to advocate for yourself as well as to avoid the snares often inherent in the ownership and leadership of family affairs.

The Conclusion reviews many of the lessons and principles that are shared in the five chapters. It also focuses on the question: who can help you, members of the rising generation, navigate your central work of individuation? We discuss two such helpers: elders and mentors. Elders help members of the rising generation through specific transitions. If you are lucky enough to find one, a mentor can help your entire life evolve.

At the end of each chapter we offer you, as a member of the rising generation, a question or questions to reflect upon. The Appendix recapitulates these questions and also provides references for other exercises and tools that you can use to guide yourself in pursuing the strategies discussed in the chapters. If you, your family, or your family's advisers would also like to plan a program to develop the capacities of the rising generation, the Appendix includes reference to a multistep curriculum that reduces the lessons of this book to a form that can be delivered and discussed over several meetings.

Again, our goal is to advance the conversation with the rising generation. Our hope is that, whatever your stage of life, you find that these pages prompt your reflection and growth, and that these chapters and these tools help your entire family rise to the challenge of fostering the flourishing of the rising generation.

Our Approach

Let's turn, then, to the conversation. We do not want to speak *about* or *to* members of the rising generation. We want to speak *with* you. Our goal is a conversation rather than a lecture. That is why each chapter of this book is short, readable on its own, and peppered with self-reflective questions. We want to give you an opportunity both to *reflect* and to *take action*. We hope to hear your full-throated voices rather than to cement your deafening silence. Most fundamentally, we want to open up for you a realm of true choice based on self-knowledge.

Our emphasis on choice is not incidental. One of the greatest sources of pain within families with wealth is the belief that there are no choices. Sometimes even wealth creators who feel very able in their businesses feel at the same time that their wealth will inevitably become a pernicious influence on their children and grandchildren. And it is not uncommon for members of the rising generation to feel that many of the important choices in their lives have been made by their parents or grandparents.

This sense of helplessness is part of the silence that we see befall rising generations, and it is a great obstacle to individual and family flourishing. Financial assets do not destroy families. A belief in our own incapacity does. This belief is what dissipates our human capital, our true asset. The way forward, then, depends on the realization that, while every family dissolves eventually, this outcome is not necessary *at this moment in time*. As common as it is for families to dissipate their wealth or even break apart, they do not have to—at least your family does not have to now, or next year, or within the next 10 or even 100 years. Despite the law of entropy, Mother Nature is kind: she says that *the shirtsleeves proverb will eventually come true, but when it does is up to you*. Families are made up of individuals, and as an individual you have choices.

This is the most important point: *you, as a member of a rising generation, have choices.* You may feel as though your life path was marked out even before you were born. This feeling may have some truth to it, especially if structures such as trusts play a large role in your family's life. But it masks a deeper truth: all these structures are external to our lives. No trust document can tell us what the right choice is. Such choices are our own. If we achieve nothing else in this book, we hope that we *encourage*—that is, give courage to—you in understanding and making these choices. In this sense, we see ourselves aligned with the character of Athena from *The Odyssey*, who appears at the beginning of the story in the guise of a family friend, and who encourages the young Telemachus to seek not only his father but, most importantly, himself. This bit of encouragement is all it takes to start an epic— if just one reader feels empowered by our pages to undertake such a journey, we have accomplished what we set out to do.

Aids to Navigation

Before turning to Chapter 1, we want to share some thoughts that we believe will help you start this voyage.

One of the most famous passages in *The Odyssey* occurs when Odysseus must steer his ship through a treacherous passage. On one side of the channel lies the voracious whirlpool Charybdis, which sucks in ships and crushes them to splinters. On the other side lurks the many-headed dragon Scylla, who will snatch and devour any sailors she can. Odysseus must steer a steady course between the two evils. It is a lesson about caution and the importance of the middle path.

We recommend that you also steer clear of two dangers that often beset families with significant wealth. They are not as dramatic as Scylla and Charybdis. But these dangers are more common than mythical monsters, and their effects are ultimately quite destructive.

The first danger that we have in mind is the tendency for families to give almost all their attention to the heroic founder of the fortune at the expense of the "next generations." This tendency is understandable. The founder is often a larger-than-life figure. Think of such historical individuals as Mayer Rothschild, Cornelius Vanderbilt, and John D. Rockefeller, or of more modern wealth creators such as Sam Walton, Karl and Theo Albrecht, Liang Wengen, Gina Rinehart, Carlos Slim, Warren Buffett, and Bill Gates. By creating great fortunes (or sometimes turning small fortunes into empires) these individuals tower above the crowd. They may also hold sway over almost every important family decision.

It is only right to give the founder or the hero his or her due. Homer named his poem the "Odyssey," after Odysseus, not the "Telemachus." But while this tendency to revere the heroic founder is understandable, if pushed too far it can do harm. As we will discuss in Chapter 1, you may easily find the founder's powerful example to be a black hole into which your own dreams and sense of self disappear. Measuring up to the founder's life can seem impossible.

It is for this reason that we recommend, to begin with, the relatively simple step that you avoid such terms as *next generation* or *next gen*. There is nothing wrong with speaking about a next generation of computer operating system or a next gen drug regimen. And these terms are common, especially among the advisers to families with significant wealth. The problem is that these terms put all the emphasis on the founder or founding generation. They subtly but powerfully indicate that the rising generation is merely what comes "next"—next to the founder, that is. As one young woman we know said at a conference when she heard herself referred to as next gen, "I don't want to be the 'next generation': I want my own generation!"

The other warning we ask that you keep in mind concerns the tendency to give too much emphasis to financial wealth. Again, this tendency is a natural one, especially in a family with significant wealth or an operating business. Great wealth brings great cares and great responsibilities. Prudent attention to your affairs or gratitude for good fortune is important. But making financial wealth the center of your attention will undermine your growth—and ultimately your family's financial future, too.

To make this danger more concrete, consider the famous proverb that we mentioned near the start of this Introduction: "shirtsleeves to shirtsleeves (or rice paddy to rice paddy) in three generations." It has been repeated in various forms in various places for many years. The proverb predicts that family financial wealth will not last. According to the proverb, the first generation creates the wealth, the second inherits it, and the third dissipates it. Anecdotal evidence and scientific studies have shown that the proverb largely holds true, even in countries or times without large estate taxes.[1]

The question, of course, is why. The proverb points to an answer in its brutal simplicity. According to the proverb, the first generation is the hero (because it creates financial wealth), the third generation is the villain (because it dissipates the financial wealth), and the second generation is a bunch of nobodies (because it neither creates nor spends). The proverb's caricatures of each generation underscore the problem that comes from focusing too much on finances. Generational differences are not black-and-white. Generations are interdependent. The third generation does not appear out of nowhere. They are the children of the second generation. The third generation's inability to live well with money may reflect something about their upbringing at the hands of the second generation. And the silent second generation is made up of children of the first. Their silence has something to do with their upbringing at the hands of the heroic generation.

The answer to this apparently necessary story of rise and fall is, while giving money its due, to give your primary attention to yourself, as a person, and your skills: your *human capital*.[2] For this reason, we also recommend, as an initial step, that you *recognize that every generation was or is, at some time, a rising generation.*

There is some evidence that families who succeed over time do so precisely because they live this truth. For example, in a study that we and our colleagues at Wise Counsel Research are conducting of 100 international families that have successfully transitioned a family enterprise of over $100 million over 100 years or more, we have found a consistent thread. Almost all of these families decided, quite consciously, at some point usually in the second or third generation, to move from focusing on building a great business and instead focus on building a great family. This step sounds simple, but it involves a great deal of work spanning, in each family, many decades. It begins with a conscious recognition that the family's true wealth is its human capital, not its financial assets.[3]

If you do nothing else that this book recommends, embrace this truth: your true wealth is your human capital—your dreams, your abilities, and your relationships. Most of us, especially when starting out in life, struggle with feeling alone. On top of that natural struggle, money has an amazing ability to make us feel isolated. It can make members of one generation feel like strangers or even enemies to members of another. But we have more in common than we often think. Look for those people in your life who can be there for you, as a person, not just as a member of a rich family. Look for those people whom you can be there for. As Athena was for Telemachus, so we want to be there for you. And we want you to be there for each other. If you do this, then rather than falling silent you will silence the proverb.

Question for Reflection

Think about the next six months or year of your life. What is an important choice that lies ahead of you in this space of time? Keep this choice in mind as you read the following chapters, remembering that you *do* have a choice.

Notes

1. See, for example, Tom Nicholas, "Clogs to Clogs in Three Generations?" *Journal of Economic History* 59(3) (Sept. 1999), 688–713.
2. Our co-author Jay Hughes's classic book *Family Wealth* (New York, NY: Bloomberg, 2004 [1997]) was the first in the field to take the momentous step of emphasizing the importance of human capital. See also, in the context of family business, Ivan Lansberg, *Succeeding Generations* (Cambridge, MA: Harvard Business Review Press, 1999).
3. Dennis Jaffe, Susan Massenzio, and Keith Whitaker, eds. *Good Fortune: Building a Hundred Year Family Enterprise*, (Boston, MA: Wise Counsel Research, Inc., 2013).

Chapter 1

Setting Sail

To Members of the Rising Generation
This chapter—indeed, this book as a whole—is meant for you.

T here are many books, and some good ones, written for your parents and grandparents. (Indeed, our previous book, *The Cycle of the Gift*, is meant primarily for them.) These books may speak about the next generation, but usually as an *object* of your parents' or grandparents' care and concern, not as a subject in your own right. You may benefit from such books, but they are not truly meant for *you*.

In this chapter, we will encourage your reflection on the challenges that family wealth poses to you—challenges often unrecognized but almost always felt. In the next chapter, we will ask you to step back and observe the characteristics and the challenges common to rising generations in general, with or without wealth. Then, in Chapters 3 through 5, we will engage you in considering strategies for dealing with these challenges and fostering your own flourishing.

Who do we mean by *you*? We mean especially members of the so-called "second generation" in enterprising families. You have grown up in the presence—perhaps the shadow—of successful parents, some who may seem larger than life. You, too, may have labored at their side but most likely under their direction. You know that they can be a tough act to follow.

By you we also intend to include members of generations beyond the second. In such cases, the founder of your family's fortune may be an old man or woman or even a picture on the wall. The stories of the founder's rise may seem like ancient history—and yet those tales and their financial consequences probably still hold a powerful place in your thoughts and actions.

Whatever your exact relationship to the founders, you, our readers, are rising within a world that those founders helped create. They likely control or have established the mechanisms for control of your family's financial capital. *But you hold the future*, and that is the greatest repository of *human* capital possible. Your task, then, is twofold: to recognize the reality of the world in which you are rising but also to rise, responsibly and happily, in a life that you create.

The Black Hole

We have referred several times to the challenges that wealth poses to the rising generation. You may wonder, "What are these supposed challenges?" After all, financial wealth is usually considered a good thing. It enables us to buy homes, pay for educations, take vacations, and help others. Most people worry about having too little, not too much.

Some of your parents, teachers, or other authorities may have summed up the problem with family wealth in one foreboding word: *entitlement*. Another common label for the problem is *dependency*. In some circles, you may even hear young members of families with wealth described as *trust babies*. These are not terms applied to wealth creators. They are usually reserved for members of the rising generation whose rising has, in the view of their parents, gone awry.

We do not deny that such words as entitlement or dependency can sometimes be useful. (Trust baby is an insult, meant to be destructive.) But these words do not, in our view, adequately describe the problem.

At the risk of oversimplifying a complicated matter, we believe that the source of the problems that family wealth poses to rising generations lies in the source of family wealth itself: the founder or, more precisely, the *founding dream*. It is the power of the founding dream that, in our view, often ends up silencing the dreams of rising generations. This silence, in turn, is the reason that the proverb of "shirtsleeves to shirtsleeves in three generations" so often comes true. It is the true cause of entitlement and dependency.

Why do we identify the source of the problem with the founder or the founding dream? Think for a moment about the founder or founders of your family's fortune. Most likely, the founder had big plans and a large sense of his[1] own ability to put those ideas to work. We call this sense of one's own ability *self-efficacy*. The founder's dream takes material shape in an idea, then a business, and then in the family's financial wealth. It projects itself into business relationships, personal relationships, and legal structures. Ultimately, the dream may inform what work family members do, whom they marry, how they raise their children, and how they spend "their" money. It likely will define the family's impact on the community—whether through business or philanthropy or both. It will give the family its name, in the sense of its public reputation.

We have seen the founding dream take shape in all these ways and more. Such a dream is almost like a sun (see Figure 1.1). It opens the eyes of colleagues, coworkers, and family members

Figure 1.1   Founder's Dream as Sun

to new possibilities. It brightens a path for their efforts. It illuminates the founder and his or her family and shows them to the rest of the world. A founder's dream is an extraordinary and impressive expression of human capital.

Such a dream is a smaller version of the great dreams of political founders or refounders, such as George Washington, Abraham Lincoln, Winston Churchill, Mahatma Gandhi, Martin Luther King, Jr., and Nelson Mandela. These founders' dreams have lit up our countries and our world. The dreams of family founders do the same on a smaller stage but with even more concentrated power.

The challenges created by such dreams are also similar in the political and the domestic realms. Thomas Jefferson thought that the "tree of liberty" must be refreshed (with the blood of patriots and tyrants) every 20 years at least—that is, by every rising generation.[2] As a young politician, Abraham Lincoln feared that the passing of the Founding Fathers would lead to political chaos, since future leaders could not imagine surpassing the deeds of Washington or Jefferson, and as a result might not even try, leaving the country rudderless.[3] Twenty-five years later, in his most famous speech, Lincoln recast the bloody Civil War as ushering in a "new birth of freedom," not just for the United States but possibly for the world.[4]

Both Jefferson and Lincoln saw the challenge posed by a great dream: precisely because of its power, the founding dream may silence the dreams of rising generations. This is the paradox of dreams. Dreams are a fundamental example of human capital. But by their power they may prevent future dreams from being born. In such cases, human capital destroys itself. The founder's sun becomes a *black hole* (see Figure 1.2).

Figure 1.2   Founder's Dream as Black Hole

In the case of families, the greater the founder's dream, the more powerful the effects of the black hole may be. Ask yourself: In what ways, in what areas of my life, do I feel the gravitational pull of the founder's dream? Do I see it at work in my parents or siblings? Do I see it at work in our choices, in our relationships, and in our plans? How do I see myself in comparison to the great man (or woman, or couple)? Have I begun to think of myself as merely "next"? Am I living in the black hole?

Talking about Silence

If some of these questions strike home, then you know the power of the founder's dream on rising generations. The fear of failing to measure up, or to strike out on your own, may outweigh the hope of future possibilities. When fear outweighs hope, the practical effect is that family members fall silent. You may come to believe that nothing you can think or say or do matters, compared to the greatness of the founders. You may believe everything is already done or decided. If so, your voice and dreams vanish into the black hole.

There are many ways that this silence can express itself. It can even be quite eloquent. Following are some examples of the forms this silence can take, examples taken from our experience but abstracted in various ways to make a point. The names are invented; the caricatures are composites. We follow each example with some questions to ask yourself.

The Very Good Steward

Hudson grew up knowing his family was wealthy. He knew about the business, the factories, the trusts, and so forth. Even in grammar school, he took pride in telling his classmates about how the stock market worked. (Most of them thought he was a bit of a show-off.) When he graduated from college, he moved into the role of serving as trustee, joining his family business's board, and generally keeping track of the family finances. His parents were delighted with his responsible behavior. As his life went on, however, Hudson's pride in himself turned into a deep sense of being burdened. He felt as though he never gave himself the chance to live his own life.

Have you ever been told, "What I really want is for you to become a good steward of our family's wealth"? There is nothing wrong with being a steward. A good steward takes care of someone else's property while that person is away. Stewardship has a distinguished history in the context of charity, in which believers are encouraged to see themselves as stewards of God's creation, to preserve it and use it for the good of the less fortunate.[5] But this is also the problem: if you are asked to become a steward, then who are you living for? Whose dream are you stewarding? Yours or the founder's? If you become a steward only of someone else's dream, then your own voice will likely fall silent.

The Meteor

When Kathy was in college, her mother pulled her aside during a visit home. Her mom said to her, "Because of your grandfather's success, I want you to know that you can do whatever you like in life." Kathy was puzzled: "I already thought I could do anything," she replied. As Kathy grew and money from her grandfather's business started to flow her way, that conversation stuck in her mind. She had always wanted to become an attorney. But after law school, the partner track seemed too constraining. She dabbled in legal advocacy but felt uncomfortable among her much-less-wealthy colleagues. Her vacations grew longer. Sure, her life was pleasant, and so she felt she could not complain. But somehow she felt that she had missed her true calling.

Do you ever feel knocked off course by your family's financial wealth? Even if you don't know its exact extent, has knowing that it is out there led you away from paths that, you suspect, might have been more rewarding? These are questions that point to the power of gifts to become, as we put it in *Cycle of the Gift*, meteors that drive recipients off their life's path. Even if that meteor comes from a place of love, it can be difficult to think and talk about this feeling of having lost your way.

Froggy

Billy had always loved boats. Growing up in a middle-class family, he dreamed of earning a captain's license and becoming a pilot. When his father's business took off, Billy found himself being given enough money to buy himself a yacht he had never even dreamed of owning. He also found himself married to someone who he realized married him only for his money. His parents continued to subsidize his life. He gave up the dream of becoming a pilot. Why bother? He had the boat already. He also stuffed down, into his unconscious, any thought of getting a divorce. He feared that a divorce would decimate his finances and that he could not make it any longer without the money. He spent more and more time on his boat, alone.

You probably know the famous image: a chef places a frog in a pot over a fire. If the water is too hot, the frog will jump right out. But if the chef slowly increases the heat, the frog will not notice the change. Once he gets uncomfortable, the frog will find his muscles are already too weakened to make the leap. He's cooked. Billy had become a frog. His parents were the chefs. The financial wealth was the flame and his marriage and lack of ambition were the pot. Financial wealth can be so comfortable: why leap out? Also, others will tell you that life outside the pot is tough and unpleasant. Why jump into that unknown, frightening world when you might have so much to lose?

The Parallel Universe

Moshe's parents worked in high-level positions in an international charitable organization. He grew up in some of the most impoverished and dangerous places in the world. He admired his parents' dedication, even if it did entail constant moves and tough living. He also knew that his mother's parents were involved in some sort of business, but he didn't know quite what it was. He certainly did not know what bearing it had on his life. Then, when he was 21, his mother brought him to a meeting of her family back in their homeland. He learned that his mother was part of one of the richest families in the country. Everything Moshe thought that he knew about himself and his family suddenly seemed turned upside down. He had thought of himself as a sibling to the poor children with whom he had grown up; he thought of himself as a true citizen of the world. Now he felt lost, his passport revoked.

Do you feel in the dark about your family's resources? Are those resources something hinted at but never quite clearly explained? Do you feel like you are living in a parallel universe—parallel to both to your parents' world and to your peers'? Your parents' money is somehow there—for example, in the beautiful houses or luxurious family vacations—but it is not yours. At the same time, when your peers without wealth face the normal struggles of making it on their own, you may not feel that those same struggles are truly yours either. This limbo-land of unreality can also instill a confused silence.

The Anxious Heir

Anna and her brother Grant knew that they were wealthy. By their 20s they had inherited hundreds of thousands of dollars from their successful parents. They were responsible young adults. Neither one of them had gotten deeply into drugs or any other trouble. After Grant got married, he told Anna that he was planning to invest a significant part of his inheritance in his wife's fledgling import-export business. He was proud of the opportunity to "do something" on his own, with his wife.

Anna, in contrast, was distraught. As she put it to a friend, she couldn't believe that Grant was going to risk "all the money he'll ever have."

If you have received some financial wealth from your family—either outright or more likely in a trust—have you ever worried that this is all you will ever have? It is a natural concern. Most recipients cannot imagine creating such great financial wealth themselves. And yet this feeling leads easily to focusing on "keeping what I've got" instead of exploring new possibilities and taking risks. It can lead to an anxious silence.

Mr. Reputable

Josef came from an old, well-known European family. He grew up hearing about the imperative of preserving the family's "good name." Josef moved to the United States, in part to be free from always being thought about in relation to his family. Even there, however, he was meticulous about his family's reputation. He kept his family history as secret as possible. Though he was trained in business, he avoided partnerships with others. He drank minimally, never touched drugs, and even avoided driving when he could. All this caution stemmed from his fear that one slip could besmirch his family's honor.

Have the founders of your family fortune bequeathed you a famous name and publicity? If so, then you have probably felt the anxiety of not wanting to stain the family reputation. Especially in this age of the Internet, continuous news cycles, fascination with celebrities—in which it seems that no mistake is ever forgotten—do you feel that there is nowhere to hide? Again, such anxiety is partly a reasonable response to a difficult situation. But it hardly encourages one to take risks in the pursuit of growth. Rather, it prompts one to quietly play it safe.

The Grand Giver

James grew up in a very wealthy family. His grandfather was at one time the richest man in his country. But James never felt comfortable with his inheritance. He felt guilty that he had so much and others had so little. In his 20s he decided to put things right by giving away the funds over which he had control. It took him about a decade to do so. While he did not regret his choice for himself, later in life he did wonder whether it was the wisest approach, particularly when he considered the options left open to his children.

Have you ever wanted to give it all away? We have known heirs who spent their fortunes on houses, cars, parties, and so on, precisely because they felt so uncomfortable with the wealth. Others gave most of it away to friends or charitable organizations in order to get out from under the burdens they felt. Such spending can appear to express a dream, especially a philanthropic one. But if the spending or the giving happens in order to negate the wealth, then is it really *your* dream?

Testing the Boundary

If the black hole and its silence have touched your life in these or other ways, do not despair. Journalists, historians, and popular writers often focus on the "dark side of wealth." But for every family that has succumbed to the black hole, there are others who have truly and effectively helped the rising generation find their voice.

The most famous example remains the Rockefellers. No one had a larger dream than John D. Rockefeller, "Senior." His son, "Junior," grew up under his father's close supervision. JDR, Jr. had a strict allowance and learned financial skills at the hands of his frugal father. But, very importantly, his father also gave him space: in his choice of career, his philanthropic efforts, and his decisions in raising his own children. Nothing would have been easier for Senior—who was no shrinking violet—to dictate to his children where they should work, whom they should marry, and how they should raise their children. But Senior did not do so. After a period of some indecision and soul searching, JDR, Jr. took advantage of his freedom, found his way, and pursued a similar path with his own children, giving them space in the important choices in their lives. As a result, while preserving a rich family history, the family has also felt the freedom to reinvent itself with each rising generation.

The Rockefeller example sheds light on the key step that a family must take in order to avert the negative outcomes of the black hole. We describe this step as continually testing the boundary. Every founding dream or black hole has its gravitational pull. For members of future generations, life within the boundary of this gravity will likely be, as one of our clients put it, "stunted." It will be the existence of the frog in the pot. The founding dream will preclude the growth of the dreams and hence the human capital of family members within the line (see Figure 1.3).

Figure 1.3   Black Hole with Boundary

So does flourishing consist in blowing through the line and speeding away from the black hole? No, as we have seen, that too can lead to silence, if that action takes the form of rejecting the family wealth—either through consumptive spending or philanthropy—in order to get rid of it. Another version of such rejection is living a stealth-wealth lifestyle: ignoring the wealth, not opening the statements from the bank or the investment company, and refusing the vacations or other trappings of an affluent lifestyle. Such rejection is not freedom. If you spend your life trying to get away from the black hole, it is still with you, always determining your attempts to reject it. Lives spent in rejection can be just as stunted as those lived within the luxurious confines of the founder's estate and vacation homes.

That is why we find a more productive option in testing the boundary or, as we sometimes call it, the "green line" around the black hole. JDR, Jr. did not reject his father's dream nor did he simply bow to it. He and many of his descendants found a balance between the powerful dreams of the founder (or the refounders) and the yet-to-be-born dreams of the future.

Another family we once worked with included a founder whose dream had involved a variety of activities, from natural resource development to finance to extreme sports. As a result, his daughters grew up with experiences all around the world and could have chosen from widely different careers, if they wanted to work within their father's companies. Thankfully, their father valued his own freedom so much that he wanted to ensure that they pursued freely chosen paths of their own. We helped each one of them identify her own dreams and the places where her dreams might intersect with or diverge from her father's enterprise. We also facilitated conversations between each daughter and her father about this process of reflection. This was work right on the boundary of the black hole, with all of its danger and its energy.

Finding your voice means neither parroting your parents nor always contradicting them. Discovering the balance is a crucial task of the rising generation.

Mentor

We began this chapter by emphasizing that we are speaking *with* you, members of the rising generation, not about you or down to you. With various questions and examples, we hope to encourage you in a conversation with yourself.

For sometimes it can be hard to face such realities as the black hole or the silence on your own. Even in the world of affluence—or perhaps especially in the world of affluence—with all its servants and helpers and advisers, you may feel alone. You may wonder, "Who is truly standing *for me* and not just for my money?"

This is not an idle question. As we will discuss in the Conclusion, most advisers to families with significant wealth or businesses also operate within the gravitational pull of that same black hole. That is why 95 percent of you, the rising generation, leave your parents' advisers as soon as you receive gifts, and 98 percent of you leave your parents' advisers once your parents have died.[6]

Who, then, stands for you? You will find such people—and the discovery often happens when you decide to stand for yourself. The story of Homer's *Odyssey* is helpful here. At the beginning of the story, Odysseus's son, Telemachus, is moping around his home, unsure of what to do. The goddess Athena appears to him in disguise. (She first appears as a traveling merchant, Mentes. Later she appears in the guise of an old family friend, Mentor, whom Odysseus had left to watch over his young son.) She asks him some tough questions. She gives him some tough criticism.

Her words rouse him from his sulk, and he decides to make a break and start a journey to find his father and himself. To begin a journey, even with help, we must be ready to receive that help. If Athena had come a year earlier, Telemachus would likely have been too young to undertake this quest. It is worth asking yourself, too, "In what ways am I ready to start this journey and what ways not?" Finally, it is worth remembering that, behind her disguise, Athena was a goddess. There is something divine about the best help. It comes to us when we are ready but not at our beck and call. You do not necessarily pick the time and the mentor. What you can do is to make yourself ready to answer the call.

Questions for Reflection

Where do you stand in relation to the black hole? Who stands for you and your freedom from its gravity?

Notes

1. When referring to the founder in the singular, we will follow convention and use the masculine pronoun, recognizing that, while most past and present founders are men, female founders are growing more and more numerous.

2. Letter from Thomas Jefferson to William Stevens Smith, November 13, 1787.

3. Abraham Lincoln, "The Perpetuation of Our Political Institutions: Address before the Young Men's Lyceum of Springfield, Illinois," January 27, 1838. Lincoln was himself only 28 years old when he gave this amazingly prescient speech.

4. Abraham Lincoln, "Gettysburg Address," November 19, 1863.

5. For more on stewardship in this context, see Paul Schervish and Keith Whitaker, *Wealth and the Will of God* (Bloomington: Indiana University Press, 2010).

6. Michael Sisk, "How to Keep the Kids," *Barron's* (June 4, 2011), S20–S21. See also Diane Doolin, Vic Preisser, and Roy Williams, "Engaging and Retaining Families," *Investments & Wealth Monitor* (September/October 2011), 10–16.

Chapter 2

Rosy-Fingered Dawn

Awakening

If you are a member of the rising generation and you have read thus far, stop for a moment and reflect. You have started a journey. You have taken a leap. You have stepped over that green line, that boundary that circumscribes the gravitational pull of the black hole of the founding dream. You are standing, now, in a position of great energy and great risk. It is a position of great energy because, like most important boundaries in life, it brings together competing and conflicting forces: past and future, constraint and freedom, tradition and innovation, to name a few. It is a place of risk because your path is uncharted. You have choices, and with choices always come risks. Appreciate the momentous nature of your step.

Several of the episodes of Homer's *Odyssey* begin with the image which has given this chapter its title: "Dawn spread her rosy fingers over the wine-dark sea." Dawn is a rising. She is also, according to Homer, a goddess, who lights up what is possible, both in terms of space—the expanse of the sea—as well as in time—the coming day with all its opportunities and challenges. Her rosy fingers are inviting, not threatening. She serves as a mediator between the gods on high Olympus and mortal men. Dawn connects the high and the low, making a whole that is visible, and intelligible, and even inviting.

We begin with this image to offer you a similar invitation. As members of the rising generation, you have begun your journey. You have considered, with us, the challenges that wealth can pose to anyone starting out on this path, in particular, the challenge of the black hole and its silence. In this chapter, we want to consider what a rising generation is. What are the characteristics enjoyed by and the challenges faced by any member of a rising generation, with or without wealth? This consideration will give us the foundation to move, in Chapters 3 to 5, to strategies for making the most of your own rising.

Rising

It may help to begin with some things that we do *not* mean when we speak of the rising generation. It is tempting to equate rising with young. While there are many points of overlap, the two are not the same. Not all who are young are rising. (And not all who are rising are young—a point that we will come back to in Chapter 5.) Too many people who are young in age have become old in spirit. The powers of the black hole, or other obstacles, have sapped their ability to rise.

Some members of the rising generation are also emerging adults. This is a new developmental stage used to describe the period from 18 to 25 or so when young people, particularly in developing countries, are neither adolescents nor full-fledged adults.[1] It is an in-between time. Most emerging adults still consider themselves learning and not settled in a career. Many still live at home but do not think of themselves as children or dependents. Very few are married or have children, but they may be in romantic relationships or even cohabitating. In line with our theme and the example of Telemachus, we often speak of emerging adults as navigating the "Odyssey years" of life.[2] As we will discuss more below, if you are a member of the rising generation who is also an emerging adult, it will be important to be conscious of these developmental characteristics and challenges while not letting them define your rise.[3]

As we mentioned in the Introduction, we also do not equate the rising with the next or second generation in a family with wealth. By being defined in reference to the primary, creative generation, the next generation finds its own voice silenced. Of course, some members do manage to speak up, but it is in spite of rather than thanks to this label of next. The same goes for the generation that is defined as second with respect to the creation of financial wealth. We hope that we can help you strip away these labels, which give priority to your parents or their money, and instead be yourself.

So if the rising generation is not simply young, or second, or next, what is it? Most fundamentally, it is an attitude or a state of mind. A rising generation is defined not by biology or finances but by psychology.

The core element of this psychology is an awareness of *growth, possibility,* and *hope.* As a member of the rising generation you recognize that you are far from finished. You may have barely begun. This does not mean that you have not accomplished much, perhaps especially in the realm of education. But behind each mountain rises another, beckoning you onward. This process of growth can be painful and frustrating; you have had and will have growing pains. A sense of possibility often brings with it some confusion, indecision, and premonition of danger. That is only human: part of our awareness of growth is the awareness of the risks that growth brings. But this is where hope comes into play. Those possibilities beckon to you rather than threaten you. Your hopes outweigh your regrets.

This hopeful awareness of the possibility of growth connects with another element in rising: a strong sense of *futurity*. It is hard if not impossible to rise without some ground to rise from. You have a past, a history—personal as well as familial. But while you may feel gratitude for what your parents have given you (and perhaps some anger over what they could not), your direction is not backward, toward them, but forward, toward the future.

Perhaps it sounds commonplace to say that the rising generation focuses more on the future than the past. But this orientation is often a reorientation that takes some work. For example, at the beginning of *The Odyssey*, Telemachus is not looking ahead to the future. He is grinding his teeth with resentment toward his father for leaving him in a tough spot. He wonders aloud if he is truly his father's son or whether his mother cheated on his father—thereby slandering both his parents. Athena, in her disguise, must give him a swift kick to move him from dwelling on the past toward planning for the future. To take another example, the philosopher Nietzsche explains that it is characteristic of youth to see the world in black-and-white and to take sides. Eventually disappointments lead the young soul to criticize itself, to doubt itself, and to take sides *against youth*. But, he concludes, "A decade later: one comprehends that all this, too—was youth!"[4] If you are still fighting the past, then you are traveling into the future with your back turned. Truly rising sometimes involves letting go of youthful resentment toward your origins and your earlier self.

Another part of rising is a desire to *struggle* or even to fight. Sometimes the most obvious thing to fight against is the past and the family from which you come. Because of the reality of this need to struggle, societies everywhere have created rituals or activities that give the rising generation a chance to do so. For example, in the near past, families with wealth offered very specific ordeals (at least for their male members), including boarding school, roughing it outdoors, and war.[5] In other, more aristocratic times and places, young gentlemen, if not away at war, would pursue their luck at the gaming tables. Such serious games were perhaps the only place where the man who can buy everything could test himself against the tough reality of success or ruin.[6] We do not mean to endorse gambling or warfare. But these pursuits met and in some places still meet a true and worthy need for the rising generation.

Finally, one of the most widely observed characteristics of the rising generation, at any time or in any place, is a desire for *connection*. People who feel hopeful draw like-minded people to themselves. Perhaps the saddest part of decline is that we retreat into ourselves; we avoid others and they tend to avoid us. The opposite happens when we are rising. The rising generation has a sort of natural charm, which is pleasing and attractive. It is no surprise that it is the rising generation that often creates new customs or new technology for staying connected.

In our work with families we have met many members of the rising generation who displayed some or all of these characteristics. As we have hinted above, however, sometimes it takes some work to let these qualities shine forth. For example, we knew one young man who went away to college with little sense of how different it would be from his hometown, where everyone knew his family and its financial success. He happily showed his new friends at school his expensive clothes and computer equipment and invited them to visit his family's several vacation homes. He was horrified when a few weeks later one of these "friends" published a story about him in the school newspaper, describing him as a vain, shallow, ostentatious "rich boy." In response, he retreated. He left school, returned home, and began to doubt that he could ever be anything apart from his family and its financial wealth.

We met with him over several sessions in which we discussed the hurt and surprise he felt at the newspaper story. Eventually, he began to be able to see how his behavior probably looked to the people at his school. He let go of judging (or fearing) them and instead focused on himself. Through our conversations he was able to affirm his abilities, his aptitude for sports, and his academic accomplishments. He reawakened his dream to study software design and to add to the growing field of social media. After a semester break, he was in good shape to transfer to a new school and start again. He was wiser and a bit sadder but he was also truly ready to rise.

If you are a member of a rising generation, then you can probably feel, in your own heart, some degree of the attitudes we have described: the awareness of growth, possibility, hope, futurity, as well as the desires for struggle and for connection. To pull these elements together, we use a model that we described in our prior book, *The Cycle of the Gift*.[7] We call this model the Four Cs as shown in Table 2.1.

The desire to grow and explore possibilities, with a sense of hope, is an expression of *commitment*. It leads to engagement and draws you away from the alienation that Telemachus felt at the

Table 2.1   The Four Cs

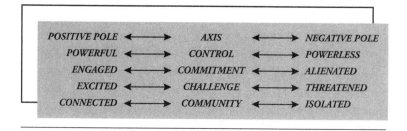

POSITIVE POLE	AXIS	NEGATIVE POLE
POWERFUL ←→	CONTROL	←→ POWERLESS
ENGAGED ←→	COMMITMENT	←→ ALIENATED
EXCITED ←→	CHALLENGE	←→ THREATENED
CONNECTED ←→	COMMUNITY	←→ ISOLATED

beginning of *The Odyssey*. The desire to face the future and to struggle is an expression of *challenge*. It leads to excitement rather than to a sense of threat or dread. From the exercise of struggling—hand-in-hand with growth and hope—grows a greater sense of *control*. This outcome leads you to feel powerful rather than powerless, master of your own life rather than the object of other people's plans. Finally, as noted above, all these activities produce a kind of charm that draws you to others and draw them to you. This *community* causes you to feel connected rather than isolated and alone.

We would invite you to take a moment here and locate yourself with respect to each of the Four Cs. Where do you stand in feeling control, commitment, challenge, and community? Do you feel more powerful or powerless? Engaged or alienated? Excited or threatened? Connected or isolated? Take a moment to use the blank space in Table 2.2 to locate yourself within the continuum of each of these four sets of characteristics.

We would add two more thoughts here concerning the characteristics of the rising generation. First, these Four Cs comprise a constellation of feelings or attitudes that also contribute to an important ability: *self-efficacy*. We mentioned self-efficacy in Chapter 1 with respect to the founders of fortunes. Self-efficacy is the sense of your own ability to make an impact in the world. It is what draws us out of our heads and into

Table 2.2   Four Cs with Blank Space

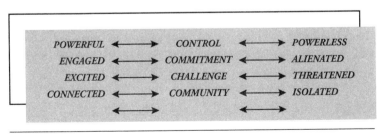

meaningful action (rather than just "spinning our wheels"). It takes some self-efficacy to begin to rise. The fullness of self-efficacy is where rising leads.

Second, the Four Cs also describe the feelings or attitudes that are central to the capacity for *resilience*. Resilience is, most simply, the ability to "bounce back" from the challenges of life, from, as Hamlet calls them, "the slings and arrows" that fortune throws our way. It is often observed that young people tend to be resilient, both physically and psychologically. This resilience is an expression of rising, the side of rising that shows itself when we meet a hurdle. A key part of rising, then, is maintaining your resilience over time and in the face of life's challenges. In Chapter 4, we focus on developing resilience in a variety of crucial areas of life.

Slings and Arrows

Some of the challenges that life throws our way are external to us and particular to our individual situations. For example, as we discussed in Chapter 1, family wealth poses challenges to members of the rising generation. The structures of family wealth can leave you feeling powerless. Wealth can also increase isolation from peers, and it may cause you to feel alienated from the regular tasks of life. This alienation may, in turn, leave you feeling threatened at the very thought of taking up meaningful struggles on your own.

But there are other challenges that beset members of the rising generation whether or not they come from families with wealth. We want to spend a moment here considering those challenges, to complete our review of what we mean by a rising generation.

Naturally, members of the rising generation may each face their own *individual* challenges that have nothing to do with money. These challenges may stem from physical, mental, or psychological limitations. None of us is perfect.

Other challenges (and opportunities!) come from our *demography*. While rising generations share many attitudes in common, each generation enters a somewhat different world. For example, much has been said and written at present about the demography of the Millennials. This is not the place for a full discussion of the differences between Baby Boomers, Generation X, and Generation Y. But a few words about Millennials may help clarify what is constant and what changes from one rising generation to the next.[8]

If you are a Millennial, then you were born between 1983 and 1996 and grew up around or shortly after the turn of the millennium. Within the United States there are about 78 million of your peers. Your attitudes were likely shaped by the terror attacks of Oklahoma City, Columbine, and September 11. You were educated by Baby Boomer parents and teachers with a heavy emphasis on self-esteem and praise rather than blame. You are the consumers and drivers of the technological trends of the present. In your life choices you tend to rank intrinsic values highest, such as work–life balance, fun, and meaning. These qualities may cause you to take on some aspects of rising (such as community and commitment) more readily than others (such as control and challenge). But do not despair: just as you are struggling with finding your way, your Baby Boomer parents are struggling just as much with the challenge of giving you the space to do so.[9]

Culture also puts a twist on the challenges faced by members of the rising generation. International observers often comment on the apparent freedom enjoyed by young people in the United States. American observers, in contrast, sometimes praise the sense of structure or purpose apparently enjoyed by many young people in the old world. Not a few people have noted that Israeli families tend to celebrate their children with a special sense of urgency, fearing that war or terrorism may snatch them away. In our work with families, we have also seen how the rising generation in many Asian families reacts differently to wealth than the rising generation in American families. One of our Asian clients once remarked, "In our families, we struggle with wealth because it feels like it gives everyone too much freedom. In your families, you struggle with wealth because it feels like it threatens to pull you too closely together." Likewise, each culture has its own rituals or processes for marking the growth of the rising generation and its transition from childhood to adulthood.

Perhaps the greatest impact on members of the rising generation comes, however, from *the variation in parents' capabilities and resources*. This is not surprising, since our parents play such a huge role in our lives, especially when we are young. We have in mind, in particular, three such capabilities.

First, there is your parents' *ability to care* for you. This ability is closely connected with your parents' *need to remain connected* with you. Some parents feel that need quite keenly. The result can be an overabundance of care, which looks, on the face of it, positive but can have long-term negative effects. Too little care and connection have obvious bad consequences: we need others' care and contact to thrive. Too much care stifles the rising generation's ability to grow. If your parents (wealthy or not) remove every obstacle or hover over every decision, then you will never build up your own strength. Healthy challenges will appear as threats. You will lack the resilience to get over inevitable disappointments. It is hard work, but for the parents out there, we hope you can separate your desire to care for, from your need to remain connected to, members of the rising generation.

Second, we have in mind a related capacity: your parents' ability to see you, their children, *for who you are* rather than as extensions of themselves. It is perfectly natural for our parents to see us as extensions of themselves. Nature (not to mention nurture) inclines us to look like, talk like, and even think or act like our parents. Still, if your parents cannot see you for who you are, it becomes extremely difficult for them to let you rise. If they cannot separate themselves from you, they may want to play out their own dreams through you. This is exactly what happens in the case of the black hole of the founder's dream within a family with wealth. The black hole almost never arises from hate or spite. Rather, it typically grows out of love. But this love is too often bound up with self-love. In some, lucky cases, the same creativity that gave birth to the founding dream also allows the founder to value the individual differences and dreams of his or her children and grandchildren.[10] But this is the exception. It is no small task for parents to learn to love themselves while also loving their children as people different from themselves.

Finally, there is what we call *parental centeredness* or *wisdom*. Parents face challenges, disappointments, and fears, too. Some of these are mundane and everyday. Others, such as the fear of death, are more episodic and profound. Through a kind of resilience or wisdom some parents are better able than others at maintaining their own centeredness or calm in the face of these challenges. Those of us who are not so able often end up unloading our anxiety or anger onto those who are closest to us: our spouses and children. Doing so unfortunately undermines the rising generation's sense of growth, possibility, and hope. It is hard to feel hopeful if you see your parents lamenting their own fates.

It is possible to do something about these challenges, but the work is usually your parents'. For example, we once worked with a man in his 50s who had been recently divorced. The separation was bitter and, for him, unchosen. He had one child, a son in his early 20s. The father called us in because of his son's behavior: he was having difficulty at school, he had fought with several friends, and he had cut off communication with his mother. While the son had his work to do, we quickly saw that his father was not making it easier for him. The father was seeking to assuage his own pain by chumming around with his son, buying him anything he wanted, and taking him on lavish vacations. Whenever the son would act out, his father would seek to fix it rather than impose consequences. The father's need for connection and his tendency to see his son as an extension of himself made it near to impossible for him to assess the young man's situation objectively. His anger at his former wife also made him volatile and left his son unsure of how his father would react to any given situation. Only through seeing the harmful effects that his neediness and volatility were having on his child was the father able to begin to regain a sense of composure. He was then able to let his son do his own work in transitioning through this challenging time of life.

The reason that these three capacities pose perennial challenges to the rising generation is that few if any of us—even when not in times of crisis, such as a divorce—are perfectly composed, balanced in our love for ourselves versus our children, and conscious of not being needy. Perhaps parents' tendency to lose their cool, be overbearing, and be needy is nature's way of prompting the rising generation to struggle to find its own way. Whatever the case may be, survey these challenges with a sense of *humility*. Psychologically, the key task of parenting and of rising is to help the members of the rising generation to *individuate*, that is, to become your own individual. Easier said than done! But just as dawn rises out of darkness, so too we hope that this survey impresses you with the possibilities and not just the challenges. After all, that is what rising is all about.

Questions for Reflection

When have you had an experience of self-efficacy? What was it like?

Notes

1. See Jeffrey Arnett, *Emerging Adulthood: the Winding Road from the Late Teens through the Twenties* (New York, NY: Oxford University Press, 2006).

2. See also David Brooks, "The Odyssey Years," *New York Times* (October 9, 2007).

3. Dr. Meg Jay argues in a recent book, *The Defining Decade: Why Your Twenties Matter—and How to Make the Most of Them Now* (New York, NY: Twelve, 2013), that the key work for emerging adults is to define their identities in such areas of work and relationships. We will focus more intently on these important areas in Chapter 4.

4. Nietzsche, *Beyond Good and Evil: Prelude to a Philosophy of the Future*, aphorism 31. The entire aphorism is a stunning reflection on the meaning of youth; the entire book is a crucial development of the concept of rising.

5. See Nelson Aldrich, *Old Money: the Mythology of America's Upper Class* (Knopf, 1988), 141–190. See Aldrich's further comments at 195: "[Old Money's] breeding in the courtesies and graces, the toughening realities of its ordeals, are supposed to lift its beneficiaries above the moral and aesthetic ugliness of the marketplace, but at the same time to discipline their freedom, giving it shape and vigor and the moral content of 'character.' Too often, however, the curriculum seems unavailing. The centrifugal force of freedom, the great double-edged gift of unearned wealth, is simply too much for it." The entire book rewards careful consideration.

6. On "serious games" see Kurt Riezler, "Play and Seriousness," *Journal of Philosophy* 38(19) (September 11, 1941), 507 and context.

7. *The Cycle of the Gift: Family Wealth and Wisdom* (New York, NY: Bloomberg, 2013), 43–44. This model rests upon the prior work of Salvatore Maddi, Suzanne Kobasa, and Dennis Jaffe.

8. For more on Millennials and wealth management, see Lisa Gray, *Generational Wealth Management* (New York, NY: Euromoney Trading, Ltd., 2010).

9. See Chip Espinoza, Mick Ukleja, and Craig Rusch, *Managing the Millennials* (Hoboken, NJ: Wiley, 2010), which, despite its focus on the workplace, offers much to parents, too; and Jane Isay, *Walking on*

Eggshells: Navigating the Delicate Relationship between Adult Children and Parents (New York, NY: Anchor, 2008).

10. For the challenges inherent in the task of fostering creativity, see Mihaly Csikzentmihalyi, *Creativity: Flow and the Psychology of Discovery and Invention* (New York, NY: Harper, 1997).

Chapter 3

Self-Knowledge

The Center

Somewhere in the midst of the wine-dark sea, according to Homer, lies the island of Ogygia. Odysseus met there the nymph Calypso, who enchanted him with her singing and detained him for seven years. She offered Odysseus immortality if he would stay. But he longed to return to his wife and family, so eventually Zeus, the father of the gods, ordered Calypso to let him go.

Homer calls Ogygia the *omphalos* or "navel" of the sea (*Odyssey* XIX.172). Calypso's name, in turn, means "hiding or hidden." The implication is that Ogygia is a spiritual center, a place that connects life with the unseen source of life.

43

The Greeks called Delphi, at the foot of Mount Parnassus, the *omphalos* or navel of the land. Neither Odysseus nor Telemachus visited Delphi, but if they had, they would have found an ancient holy place, which in time was dedicated to the god Apollo. Over the door of his temple was written the command, *Gnothi Sauton*: "Know Thyself."

This central chapter takes up that command, with special attention to knowing yourself as a member of the rising generation. In the two prior chapters, we spoke about your situation generally. Now we want to encourage you to reflect on yourself as an individual. This reflection will provide the foundation for your growth and flourishing, which we will address further in Chapters 4 and 5 and the Conclusion.

Sometimes people criticize the pursuit of self-knowledge as navel-gazing. We do not mean to encourage you to stare at your belly-button. But this rebuke captures a bit of truth. Self-knowledge demands, and leads to, a sort of calm or centeredness. The navel marks your core, the seat of stability. It also reminds you of your origin, which precedes self-consciousness. Self-knowledge never lies far from both the obvious and the mysterious in life.[1]

Internal and External

In our heads, each of us carries about an image of ourselves that we reach for in answer to the question, "Who am I?" That image may change somewhat over time, but usually it has a lasting core, which is built up on the basis of experiences, accomplishments, disappointments, and beliefs. It is the starting point for the journey of self-knowledge.

It is also a problem for that journey. This self-image is not a mirror. It may show you to yourself the way you would like to be. Sometimes it may present a version of yourself as less attractive, less intelligent, or less capable than you truly are. It is shaped by your passions—hopes, fears, love, sadness, and anger, among others. But you want to know your*self*, not an image created by yourself.

To deal with this difficulty, we encourage you to divide the task of self-knowledge into two parts. First, consider those factors that make you who you are that are *internal* to you. Then turn to those factors that are *external*. This is not a perfect division, since people can internalize external factors and sometimes project internal realities onto external objects. But it will help you get started.

Dreams

In Chapter 1, we talked about the danger that the founding dream can pose to rising generations in families with wealth. In Chapter 2, we discussed how every rising generation is characterized by its own hopes, possibilities, or, in other words, dreams. It seems right to start our consideration of internal factors by asking, "What are your dreams?"

Take a moment to think about this question. We don't pretend that it is an easy one. When children are young, they often find it easy to express their dreams, whether it is to become a firefighter or a prima ballerina. As we get older, talking about our dreams often becomes more difficult. Some people are lucky to feel always drawn to a particular pursuit. But most of us are like a young 20-something we once asked this question of. He responded, "Everyone tells me to pursue my dreams. But what if I don't know what my dreams are?" He was worried that he had already failed.

Of course, he had not. A dream is not something we pick out in a store, or find in a deck of cards, or inherit from our parents. Perhaps the best description of a dream is a calling or a *vocation*. A dream is not something you simply choose. It calls you.

For example, that same 20-something whom we mentioned above had a younger sister who had always wanted to be a doctor. In particular, she wanted to become a specialist in pediatric cardiology. This call had come to her when she was herself still a child. It puzzled her parents at the time (who were not doctors), but they let her pursue her unusual interest. Eventually, she studied premedicine in college and went on to medical school and medical research in this field. Her family's financial wealth allowed her to live in somewhat more comfortable circumstances than most medical students or interns do, but it did not get her into these programs. Most importantly, it did not give her this calling.

Sometimes the call comes earlier, sometimes later. Usually, it does not come as a voice from the sky. It evolves over time. Consider what activity or activities you have felt most drawn to in your experience. When have you felt most alive? What activities cause you to forget the time and feel "flowing," whether in action or in study?[2] Recall the Four Cs and the distinction of "Challenge versus Threat" (see Table 3.1). Which of your activities would you put at the Challenge end of the spectrum? Which at the other?

These questions may not suddenly reveal your dream. But they may reveal or underscore pursuits that will lead you closer to your dream. Some of your answers may point toward leisure activities you enjoy. Others may point toward work that intrigues you but that you have never seriously considered taking on.

Another way to explore your dreams is to reflect on any activities in which you chose to undertake an apprenticeship, that is, a demanding period of training that requires following other

Table 3.1   Modified Four Cs

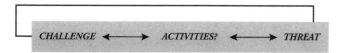

people's direction. (We have more to say on apprenticeship and its relation to work in Chapter 4.) For example, a young woman we knew always thought that she should become a professional: a doctor, lawyer, or the like. But every summer she eagerly went to camp and spent her time there learning survival techniques, forestry, and animal husbandry. Even though these camp experiences were very demanding, she thought of them just as "fun." When the summer ended, she would head back to her "serious" schooling with a heavy heart. Thankfully, as she progressed into her 20s, she realized that she had already served as an apprentice in a field where her skills could be appreciated. She took up work with an Outward Bound–type organization and found herself loving every minute of it. Again, her family's financial resources made it possible for her to attend those camps and then to give up the professional track without becoming destitute. But those resources did not give her the dream and the will to pursue it.

In reflecting on the questions we have just posed, the point here is not to judge your responses but to use them to collect data about yourself. Some questioning or skepticism about your activities or even your dreams is healthy; it is a sign of maturity. Cynicism, in contrast, cuts you off from serious attachment to work, relationships, and dreams.[3] In the end, it is important to remember that for many of us, a dream is not an answer. It is a question that continually leads us closer to what truly matters, which may itself evolve and change over time.

The great poem "Ithaca" by C. P. Cavafy makes this point. In this poem, Cavafy addresses a would-be Odysseus, who is setting out to find his way back to his home, the island of Ithaca:

> *When you set out on the journey to Ithaca,*
> *pray that the road be long,*
> *full of adventures, full of knowledge.*

This beginning is counterintuitive: Wasn't the length of Odysseus's wandering a bad thing? This belief—that the journey should be swift—matches the expectation that members of the rising generation sometimes place upon themselves (or find placed upon them): that I should know my dream and be living it now, and if I'm not, I'm a failure.

The poet then catalogues some of the wonderful sights, sounds, and even smells that the listener may encounter in his or her journey. He concludes:

> *Always keep Ithaca in your mind.*
> *To arrive there is your final destination.*
> *But do not rush the voyage in the least.*
> *Better it last for many years;*
> *and once you're old, cast anchor on the isle,*
> *rich with all you've gained along the way,*
> *expecting not that Ithaca will give you wealth.*
> *Ithaca gave you the wondrous voyage:*
> *without her you'd never have set out.*
> *But she has nothing to give you any more.*
> *If then you find her poor, Ithaca has not deceived you.*
> *As wise as you've become, with such experience, by now*
> *you will have come to know what Ithacas really mean.* [4]

Ithacas are your dreams. You do not start there. You begin far away from your destination. Sometimes you can but dimly see or imagine Ithaca. The point, Cavafy says, is the journey, not the destination. Ithaca, your dream, gives you a reason to pursue this "wondrous voyage." And the wealth you gain—in the form of experience, not money—is the voyage itself.

Strengths and Hurdles

To continue this focus on internal factors, think next about your strengths. What are you good at? What do others praise you for? Where have you enjoyed the greatest success? You decide what *greatest* means: it could be in the eyes of the world. It could be a deeply private, personal achievement. We have known members of the rising generation who define their greatness in terms of sports or academic achievements. We have known others who define it in terms of their love for their siblings or their kindness to friends.

Each of us has strengths. Part of the work of self-knowledge is not only to identify our strengths honestly but also to give them their proper place. Our educational system places a great deal of weight on self-esteem, which means that many of us grow up hearing lots about our strengths (real or apparent). This emphasis helps avoid the psychic pain that comes from criticism or blame. But it can also have the effect of orienting us too much to external rewards.

There are two problems with doing so. First, the strengths that others praise in us may not be the characteristics that will make us happiest in life. For example, a young woman we knew heard many times from her parents that her caring, conscientiousness, and attention to detail would someday make her a great president of their foundation. But what if these same strengths would have made her an even happier doctor? Second, external rewards can provide only so much satisfaction, and that satisfaction tends to decline over time.[5] Do not let yourself be penalized for your virtues.

Moving from strengths, what are the internal hurdles to your flourishing? Do you carry around *beliefs* that hold you back? Each of us holds deep-seated beliefs about ourselves as well as the world around us. For example, a young man we knew sincerely believed that if he left home and went out on his own, he would not be able to make it, to keep the lifestyle he had enjoyed. A young woman once told us, after many sessions of talking in a very guarded fashion, that she feared that others only spent time with her for her money, not for who she was. These beliefs— such as "I'm not good enough" or "People love my money, not me"—which most of us often do not even think about, in turn give rise to thoughts, feelings, and behaviors. Clarifying these deep-seated beliefs is not an easy task. It takes time and reflection.

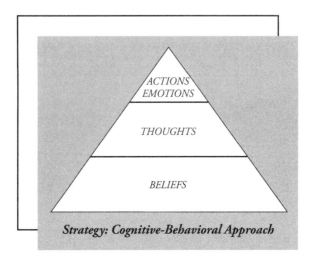

Figure 3.1   The Cognitive-Behavioral Triangle

One way to start that reflection is to observe your own behaviors and your feelings. They are like the tip of the iceberg of your beliefs (see Figure 3.1). What do they say about your beliefs about yourself and the world? The same goes for your automatic thoughts, the ideas or statements that rise into your head without any effort. What do they tell you? From these observations you can then turn to your beliefs themselves. Some questions that may help in that reflection include:

- What do you believe about yourself? Are you your own best friend or your own worst enemy? Do you believe yourself able to take on the challenges of life? Or do you find yourself believing that you are not up to it?
- What do you believe about the world? Is it a trusting and safe place? Is it a place where people help each other? Do you believe that things get better or worse over time?
- Do your beliefs help you or hurt you?

Individuation

So far, we have been focused on the internal *content* of identity (dreams, strengths, and hurdles). It is also important to reflect on the internal *process* of growth. Who you are changes as you develop through life. Locating yourself within the process of development is part of self-knowledge.

A helpful description of development is offered by psychoanalyst Erik Erikson, in his eight developmental life stages.[6] Each stage is characterized by a conflict or crisis that must be resolved before we can successfully move on to the next stage of development. Over years of working with families, we have adapted Erikson's list of stages into the following steps, each with a list of characteristic activities or milestones:

Breaking Loose

Leaving home, focusing on peers, testing your wings, loneliness, attachment to causes, changing lifestyles, challenging family morals, conforming to new friends.

Building the Nest

Search for identity, intimate friends, marriage, intoxication with own power, great dreams, making commitments, taking on responsibilities, getting launched into a career, working toward goals, doing "shoulds," finding a mentor, having children.

Looking Around

Raising questions, recognizing painful limitations, gathering possessions, moving up the career ladder, possible declining satisfaction in marriage, settling down, desiring freedom, asking "What do I do with my life?"

Midlife Rebirth

Awareness of mortality, diminished physical energy, emotional turmoil, parenting teenagers, finding new friends, deep questions, changing careers, second adolescence, sense of aloneness, possible divorce, remarriage, conflicting pressures, remodeling life structures, learning to play again.

Investing in Life

Life reordered, settling down, acting on new values, focus on people instead of possessions and power, cultivating a few good friends, last child leaving home, grandparenting, more financial freedom, enjoying life, empty nest, lost dreams.

Deepening Wisdom

Softening feelings, mellowing wisdom, steady commitments to self and others, deepening richness, simplifying life, adjusting to limitations, loss of energy, financial pressures, retirement, quiet joys, self-knowledge, self-acceptance, facing death.

Twilight Years

Loneliness, freedom from shoulds, dependence on those who once depended on you, mind sharp/body failing, body fine/mind failing, loss of mate and friends, preparing for death, sense of peace and perspective.

As you review these stages, think about and briefly answer the following questions:

- What stage of adult development are you in right now?
- What stage of development are the significant others in your life in?
- What special challenges are you experiencing in your present stage of development and how do you plan to address them?

Many of you, our readers in the rising generation, are likely in one of the first three stages listed above. This is the time of life when the key work, vis-à-vis your family, is to *individuate*. Individuation involves both separating from your family of origin (sometimes geographically, socially, and even in terms of your beliefs or practices) and also establishing your own individual identity.

Individuation involves a tricky balance. Separation is not abandonment. It does not mean leaving your family of origin behind. Establishing your own individual identity usually entails deconstructing and then reconstructing that family relationship. The rocky times of adolescence and young adulthood are all part of the process of eventually coming back together as adults.[7]

This balancing act is often made more difficult when wealth is a significant part of a family's life. The founding dream may leave little room for establishing an individual identity that you feel proud of. Also, trusts, businesses, family compounds, family philanthropies, and the like may make it hard to separate. In working- or middle-class families, separation may happen as a matter of course: getting out into the world is more attractive than living in Mom and Dad's basement.

In contrast, growing up within a family with wealth may insulate members of the rising generation from not only the need to individuate but also the knowledge of the very possibility of individuation. Remember the image of the frog that we used in Chapter 1. The frog's problem in the slowly heated pot is that he is not even aware of himself and his environment. The pot is comfortable (at least for the moment). He is relaxed in the warmth. He may be bored and inert, but there seems no need to jump away. Just imagine if that frog were also being fed tasty treats while the pot warms up. It would be surprising if he did decide to leap out into the cold world before he was completely cooked.

With this image in mind, take a moment to ask yourself: Do I know what it means to individuate? Are there examples I can look to (in my family, among my friends) of people who have successfully individuated? What does becoming my own individual person look like to me?

Externals

What goes on in your head comprises perhaps the most important factors in making you who you are. But the outside world plays a role, too. In seeking to know yourself, consider too these external factors:

- *Geography*. Where did you grow up or are you growing up? How did the people or customs there shape your thinking? Thinking ahead, where do you think you could find the greatest happiness?
- *Demography*. When did you grow up? What were the public events that most shaped your memories?
- *Family*. Are your parents able to separate out their need for connection from their desire to care? Do they see you as an individual or as an extension of themselves? Do they present you with an example of calm and centeredness?
- *Social life*. Who are your true friends? What kind of people are they? What parts of you do they bring out?
- *Financial wealth*. If there is financial wealth in your family, when did you first become aware of its presence? Was that experience a positive or a negative one? In what ways has the money made your life better? In what ways has it been problematic?[8]

In response to this last question, we have found the diagrams in Figures 3.2 through 3.4 helpful, to clarify the extent to which you are stewarding someone else's dream or living your own.

The first circle shows the norm of balance between your family's dreams and your own. The second shows what often happens: the founding dream overpowers and almost extinguishes the individual's dream. Some people may find the third circle attractive, as the individual dream overshadows the founding dream. In truth, at different points in life, the founding dream may appropriately loom larger, at other points smaller. The yin-yang suggests that it is never possible for either part—your

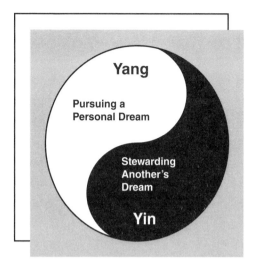

Figure 3.2   The Yin-Yang of the Second Generation's Journey

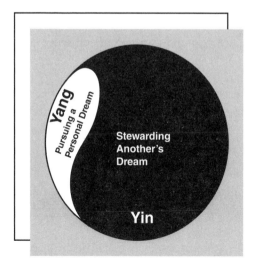

Figure 3.3   The Yin-Yang Dilemma Leading to Lack of Freedom and Suffering

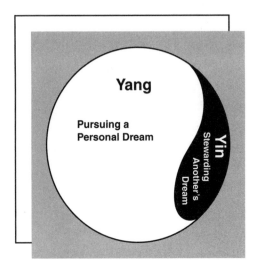

Figure 3.4   The Yin-Yang Dilemma Leading to Greater Freedom and Happiness

family's dreams or your own—to vanish completely. A key task of individuation is finding a balance, wherever you are now, between where you come from and where you are going.

The Balance Sheet

We hope that the questions and exercises in this chapter help you come to deeper self-knowledge. It helps to have some way to record your insights and to measure your progress. To those ends, we have adapted the Family Balance Sheet that Jay Hughes first shared with readers almost 20 years ago.[9] The enduring worth of this tool shows that tools may be revised, but human nature and needs remains constant over time.

The goal of a balance sheet is to show the relationship between assets and liabilities. If the assets exceed the liabilities, then there is "equity"—a positive result. If the liabilities exceed, then equity is negative and bankruptcy looms. Most balance sheets are financial.

Table 3.2 Individual Balance Sheet

ASSETS	LIABILITIES	EQUITY
Your dreams?	*Others' dreams overpowering your own?*	*Growth (Despair)*
Your strengths?	*Your hurdles?*	*Self-efficacy (Impotency)*
Positive beliefs?	*Negative beliefs?*	*Resilience (Rigidity)*
Individuation?	*Enmeshment?*	*Independence (Dependency)*
Geography positive?	*Geography limitations?*	*Net?*
Demography positive?	*Demography limitations?*	*Net?*
Parents positive?	*Parental limitations?*	*Net?*
Friends positive?	*Friends' limitations?*	*Net?*
Money positive?	*Money negative?*	*Net?*
"Testing the boundary"?	*In the "black hole"?*	*Rising (Declining)*

The Individual Balance Sheet in Table 3.2 focuses on qualitative rather than quantitative aspects of life. Spend a few moments considering the preceding template and filling in what you can of your own balance.

After you have done this exercise, look at the items you list under your equity. How many are positive? How many negative? It is important to recognize here that most of us focus much more intently on our perceived faults or failings than on our strengths or other positive attributes. We call this tendency *selective negative focus*. We encourage you to do the opposite, and give yourself the permission to employ *selective positive focus,* with an emphasis on moving forward to grow your assets and address your liabilities in a productive way.

To that end, using your equity column, try creating a paragraph that summarizes the equity you have in your own human capital. This summary can serve to remind you of how far you have come—and also of areas where you would like to grow. You will also now have a record, at this moment in time, of your individual balance sheet, to which you can refer in the future when you do this exercise again.

Sometimes when we are working with a family, we invite the family members to fill out their balance sheets as a group, within the context of a family meeting. For example, we worked with one family that included two parents and four adult children in the Odyssey years of life. First, we met individually with each of them, learning about their respective views and concerns, and discovering that the development of the family's human capital was their shared goal. Then, we brought them together in a family meeting in which we gave each of them the individual balance sheet and asked them to spend 10 minutes to write down their thoughts. After that step, we broke them into three sets of two each. Within each group one member took 5 minutes to share a summary of his or her balance sheet while the other listened. In the next 5 minutes, the listener spoke and the first speaker listened. After this session, we brought them back together as a group and asked each person to share what he or she heard from the other member of their two-person group. We also gave each family member a chance to add to what his or her listener shared. We took notes while each person spoke, and after this trip around the table, we and the family spent about an hour incorporating these notes into a summary statement of the family's human capital balance sheet. The outcome was impressive, in terms of family members' educational accomplishments, work experiences, relationships, and, above all, their dreams. But even more powerful was the chance for them to listen to one another, to understand one another, and to affirm one another. This exercise laid the foundation for much impressive individual work and many successful family meetings in the years to come.

Question for Reflection

What is an example of a belief you hold about yourself, others, or the world that gives you strength?

Notes

1. This chapter offers you, as a member of the rising generation, a beginning to the path of education about yourself. For further depth, along with descriptions of specific tools that you can use to assess your own educational style, see Chapter 19 of Jay Hughes's *Family, the Compact Among Generations* (New York, NY: Bloomberg, 2007), 221–231.

2. Mihaly Csikszentmihalyhi, *Flow: the Psychology of Optimal Experience* (New York, NY: Harper, 2008).

3. For more on the difference between skepticism and cynicism, see Hughes's *Family, the Compact Among Generations*, pp. 258–259.

4. C. P. Cavafy, *The Collected Poems*, E. Sachperoglou, trans. (New York, NY: Oxford, 2007), 37–39.

5. See, for example, Daniel Kahneman and Angus Deaton, "High Income Improves Evaluation of Life but Not Emotional Well-Being," *PNAS* 107(38) (September 21, 2010), 16489–16493.

6. See Erik Erikson, *Childhood and Society* (New York, NY: Norton, 1993); Erik and Joan Erikson, *The Life-Cycle Completed* (New York, NY: Norton, 1998); and C. G. Jung, *Symbols of Transformation*, Gerhard Adler and R. F. C. Hull, trans. (Princeton, NJ: Princeton University Press, 1977).

7. For more on the work of "deconstructing and reconstructing" family, financial, and legal relationships, see our colleague Thayer Willis's book, *Beyond Gold: True Wealth for Inheritors* (Portland, OR: New Concord Press, 2012).

8. For a helpful and profound exploration of this particular question, see our colleague Jim Grubman's recent book, *Strangers in Paradise: How Families Adapt to Wealth across Generations* (Sarasota, FL: Family Wealth Consulting, 2013).

9. James E. Hughes, *Family Wealth* (New York, NY: Bloomberg, 2004), 57–61.

Chapter 4

Facing the Waves

Getting Away

After being inspired by the goddess Athena to search for his father, Telemachus assembles the noblemen of Ithaca. He gives them a speech urging them to support his quest. He assumes that his position as Odysseus's son and heir will sway them. A few of his father's old friends listen, but for the most part the lords laugh at Telemachus and even threaten to silence him. Telemachus realizes that by speaking up he put himself in danger. He secretly steals away from Ithaca that night and travels to the mainland of Greece to look for Odysseus himself.

Telemachus learns a great deal in his unplanned journey. He develops bravery in the face of danger. He learns the importance of respecting others' beliefs and practices. Perhaps based on his painful experience at home, he develops a remarkable tact and ability to converse politely with the lords and ladies whom he visits. For someone who grew up isolated,[1] he fosters an admirable friendship with several of the other young people he meets. Since he must depend on the goodwill and hospitality of others, he learns humility. Since he leaves home in a rush, he learns also to rely on himself.

Perhaps the greatest lesson for us from Telemachus's journey is that, to develop these abilities, Telemachus needed to *get away*. He was in danger at home, not only from his father's rivals but also from his own complacency. He was unhappy. But he had little opportunity or incentive to improve his situation. He was like the frog in the pot. He was inert, even in his discomfort.

This chapter will move from the pursuit of self-knowledge to the development of *resilience*. The two go together. It is hard to develop resilience if you do not know your strengths, weaknesses, and dreams. In turn, facing challenges and developing resilience teaches you a great deal about who you are.

Telemachus's example is relevant to this topic not only because much of his journey consists of his surmounting challenges and developing new abilities. He also reminds us that such development requires space. Sometimes well-meaning parents will send their children to various programs or boot camps to learn new skills. These programs have some utility. But they usually operate within the gravity of the black hole, especially when they are paid for out of the resources of the black hole and the attendees have no emotional or financial skin in the game. Learning practices or skills that you are only vaguely interested in with regard to wealth you do not consider your own inspires silence, not resilience. There is another way, but it requires that you, like Telemachus, first take a leap and set out for yourself.

Taking the Leap

What does that leap look like to you? Before we share our thoughts about ways for you to develop resilience, take your bearings from yourself. The goals here are for you to become your own person, feel capable, and rise. What do *you* think you need in order to pursue those goals resiliently?

It may be that, like Telemachus, what you need now most of all is a little space. This is sometimes hard for parents to understand. One of our clients captured the challenge for herself in this image. Parents always want to protect their children, sometimes going to great lengths to do so. They see their children as acrobats, flying through the air on a trapeze, from one challenge to the next. They want to minimize their risks, make sure their timing is perfect, and always be there to catch. But, this client said, what most parents forget is that it is at that moment when she lets go of one swinging trapeze and sails to another that the acrobat feels most free. If parents eliminate all the risks, then they will eliminate that moment of freedom, too.

That moment of freedom is what allows the acrobat to grab the next bar. Your leap into your own life beyond the gravity of the black hole is an expression of that freedom. Resilience is its continual reaffirmation.

Work

When it comes to the rising generation and wealth, work is a topic that comes up frequently but is largely misunderstood. We try to simplify matters by starting out with two important points.

First, when we talk about work within the context of financial wealth, we are talking about a very special case: the case of pursuing work without the *need* to make money, that is, without the spur of economic necessity that prompts most people to work. Even if your parents do not plan to leave you all their wealth, even if—like Warren Buffett or Bill Gates—they plan to leave you "only" a few million or a few hundred thousand dollars, or even if they have provided you with a debt-free start to life, such an inheritance goes far beyond the economic starting point for most of the world's inhabitants. Warren Buffett used to say that he planned to leave his children "enough so that they could do anything but not so much that they could do nothing." It is a laudable goal. But even this moderate position removes much of the economic necessity for work. It is important to acknowledge this reality from the beginning if it is the reality you are operating within.

Second, when we talk about work, we have in mind the great psychoanalyst Sigmund Freud's dictum that the two primary motivations in human life are "love and labor."[2] (We will take up love in the next section of this chapter.) Freud's insight reveals that labor is not just about a wage. Work is central to a flourishing human life, quite apart from its economic output. It is part of your human reality even if it is not part of your economic reality.[3]

Given these two points, the practical question is this: how can you meet your *human* need for work without laboring under the *economic* need to earn your bread?

Answering this question wisely is made all the more difficult because our contemporary world is itself confused about the meaning of work. On the one hand, there are many people today who would turn pretty much any activity into a form of work. We have knowledge workers. Parents work at home. Children's job is to do well at school. We must all work on our relationships. The whole of life is work. On the other hand, many people want to dissolve the boundary between work and personal satisfaction. Our jobs should be fun. Companies offer their employees not only breaks, but also massages, Ping-Pong tables, and group outings. Many people believe that their work should above all be meaningful, in the sense that it should bring them deep personal satisfaction and reflect their own sense of purpose. In this vision of work, the drudgery of serving others' needs seems mysteriously to fade away.

As with any confused situation, both sides of this situation speak some truth. The task, then, is to answer the practical question as thoughtfully as possible, given your own situation and abilities.

To help you do so, we offer the following definition of work, not as a last word but as a suggestive guide to your thinking and your choices: *work is any activity that challenges you and tests your abilities, that requires your dedication, and that also meets the true needs of others.* In what follows we will offer some further thoughts on each of these points, along with some stories to illustrate what we mean.

Most basically, work is *challenging.* For some members of the rising generation, the first challenge of work may be for you to get away from the parental nest and answer to people to whom you are not related and whom you may not even like. Summer jobs are a tried-and-true way to gain this experience. The challenge of work may also entail admitting your own lack of skills and accepting the rather meager compensation that a lack of skills brings. But this is where you can experience the positive side of meeting a challenge. Even if you do not need the money, a small paycheck carries with it an inestimable value: it is truly your own. You earned it.

If you keep in mind the need for work to challenge your abilities, you can also avoid some difficult situations that families with wealth often find themselves in. For example, sometimes parents will create position in their family office or family foundation for a member of the rising generation who, in their view, has not yet found him- or herself. Other times, such a position is treated as a consolation prize. These actions equate work with a position, title, and stipend. This work may be only make-work, or it may involve challenges that are not aligned to the challenges that you need to face at that point in your life.

A common case of this sort is the work of stewarding your family's assets. We know a young woman, an Ivy League grad, MBA, who earned a top role in her family's business. When it was sold, she took on the role of steward of the family wealth. "After all, someone has to do it!" she would say. Such work does demand responsibility and integrity. It combines self-interest with a laudable concern for your parents, siblings, and future generations. It gave this woman a nice-sounding title, access to investor conferences at luxurious locations, and the respectful attention of all sorts of advisers who wanted her business. And yet she came to doubt that this work truly engaged her full capacities. It left her bored. Stewardship is noble work, but is it your work?

A similar situation can arise around family foundations. One family we knew sold their successful technology company, which left their daughter, who had overseen operations, without a position. She drifted for a few months until her parents announced that she would be the new president of their foundation. At first she struggled. Dealing with the qualitative, "soft measures" of philanthropy was far removed from the quantitative, tangible inputs and outputs that she was used to. Luckily, she had some humility, and she set herself to learning about and truly understanding the motivations and needs of people on both sides of the philanthropic world (the givers and the recipients). She adapted to her work, found the challenge in it for her, and did not let it remain merely a consolation.

The key point here is not to avoid work in your family's foundation, business, or family office. Sometimes that work can be a great fit. Rather, it is to seek out work that truly challenges your abilities. If a position is a sinecure—a safe source of revenue and a title without a real connection to your own dreams and passions—then it will not meet your own human need to do good work.

Besides being challenging, work also requires *dedication* and training or what used to be called *apprenticeship*. The traditional path of work was from apprentice (who follows a master), to journeyman (who has the license to work independently) to master (who can both work on his own and teach others). This path still exists to some degree in various crafts and in the noble professions of law, medicine, teaching, and the ministry. In other areas, apprenticeship can take a variety of forms. The task is to find the form appropriate to the work you are seeking to do and to embrace it.

For example, one young man we know, when he was a junior in college, worked as an assistant to his college president. When he started the job, he imagined that he would be writing important speeches and policy papers. Instead, the president had him write thank you letters and get well notes. Over time, he allowed his young assistant to draft more substantial correspondence and even speeches. Although he had plenty of demands on his time, the president made copious notes on the young man's drafts, often requiring him to rewrite the same letter or short speech four, five, or even six times. It was a true compositional workout. Even though this young man did not go into the field of higher education administration, his apprenticeship greatly benefited his later work. It taught him humility, dedication, endurance, attention to detail, pride in a good product, and respect for superior abilities—as well as English grammar.

Families with operating businesses often intuitively appreciate the importance of apprenticeship. We know one family with a commercial real estate business that would round up the members of the rising generation to paint apartments and make minor repairs. Another family with a liquor distributorship would call all the cousins in the warehouse during the preholiday busy season to pack and unpack merchandise. Neither of these families saw this work as necessarily leading to positions within commercial real estate management or liquor distribution. They did see these tasks as training in dedication that would benefit whatever careers the members of the rising generation chose.

That said, families with operating businesses or wealth can sometimes be tempted to "help" members of the rising generation skip the stage of apprenticeship. We have known instances where families have offered their recent college graduates executive positions within their family businesses. Or, even more dramatically, parents sometimes offer adult children in their late teens or 20s the chance to start their own businesses using the family's financial capital. Usually, these offers are not made based on business calculations. Rather, parents tend to assume that taking such a job or undertaking a start-up will by themselves instill good habits and promote good character.

For example, we knew an entrepreneur who had achieved great success within the world of manufacturing product packages. He was devoted to his son, whom he hoped would someday become an entrepreneur himself. He gave his son everything the young man wanted. In turn, his son struggled in school. He did not like to finish assignments and eventually decided to skip college. Naturally, with such credentials, he could not find a job he wanted on his own. So his father gave him millions of dollars to start his own manufacturing company, with dad as chairman. It was not a success, financially or for their relationship.

None of this is meant to deny that sometimes members of the rising generation show entrepreneurial abilities even at a young age. This is not surprising. Research suggests that elements of entrepreneurship are genetic, and the entrepreneurial gene can reproduce itself within successful families.[4] But even if you have this gene, it does not invalidate the importance of apprenticeship. Indeed, it makes it all the more important. That is why many family businesses that have succeeded over generations adopt as a best practice the requirement that any member of the rising generation who wishes to join the business must first spend at least a few years working and earning promotions elsewhere.[5] Succeeding in a senior position takes much more than having the right last name. Likewise, starting a new business takes much more than money. These activities require years of preparation. Trying to step right into such roles with no real experience would be like Telemachus's trying to rule Ithaca as king without going on his own odyssey first.

To sum up this point, work cannot be mastered without apprenticeship, and it cannot be enjoyed without mastery.[6] Never serving as an apprentice in any field is a prescription for becoming a dilettante, someone who finds it hard to stay long enough with any one activity to find the true accomplishment in work.

The third characteristic of work that we highlighted above is that it *meets the true needs of others*. By this point we mean not just that you may work *for* others in the sense of report to them—after all, you may decide to be self-employed—but rather that true work *benefits* others. It is not just *self*-entertainment. Whether it is investment banking, public relations, scientific research, medicine, or social work, work produces some good that others value. That is what makes it work: *other* people find it valuable. Even the most solitary or apparently self-interested workers—such as investment analysts poring over spreadsheets—produce some value that others want. That is why their company or clients pay them. In contrast, consider sports. Sports are challenging and require apprenticeship or training. But unless you are a professional athlete, sports meet your own desire for pleasure, relaxation, and fitness, not others' needs. What distinguishes work from recreational sports is that work puts others' goods and others' needs ahead of your own. That is what makes it work—in the sense of being practical—and work—in the sense of being taxing or hard. It is hard to think about what others need and to put their needs ahead of, or at least on par with, your own.

It is especially important to remember this point when you have grown up within a family with financial wealth. Within such a world, you may be more used to others doing things for you than doing things for others. Also, affluent parents tend to want to give their children the experiences of enrichment whenever they can. So instead of working at summer or after-school jobs, you may have spent your time at camps, music lessons, sport clinics, and the like. There is nothing wrong with such activities: they can be truly beneficial to your development. But if enrichment deprives you of the opportunity to work for others, it can also deprive you of a sense of what work is all about. It can become not enriching but impoverishing. Living within this world can also make you forget that no society has ever tolerated for long a completely leisured class—that is, a class that serves only its own desires and not the good of others. Work, mutually beneficial give and take, is what holds markets and societies together.

This is why members of rising generations within families with financial wealth sometimes find themselves criticized for being professional students. It is not unusual to find family members who are on their fifth or sixth year of college or their second or third graduate degree. Again, education is a wonderful thing. But if you find yourself drifting in your studies, it is important to ask yourself, "Am I pursuing this education because I think it will allow me to live a better life and do good for others, too? Or am I avoiding something?" After all, there is a big leap between the classroom and a real-world job. In the classroom, we are surrounded (we hope) by well-meaning teachers who are trying to teach us for our good. At a job, we are expected to use our learning and our abilities to benefit others. The difference is not just between theory and practice. It is the difference between serving our own good and serving others' good.

To make this distinction concrete, we recall a young woman from a family with significant financial wealth who wanted to become a teacher. By her mid-20s her only experience teaching was in the relatively controlled environment of graduate-school practicums. She decided to test herself and found a job in an inner-city school—the best job she could find with her relatively limited experience. Teaching in that school was tough. The students, their families, her colleagues, and the physical environment were unlike anything she had known in her affluent upbringing. But she stuck with it and developed great resilience as a teacher and as a young woman. She realized that, as enjoyable as it is to be a student, true fulfillment in her work required stepping out of the cocoon of educating herself and into the challenge of educating others.

This example also sheds some light on what your parents can do to help you, members of the rising generation, to do your work and face your challenges. This young woman's parents could have easily given her an allowance that would have outstripped her paycheck as a fledgling teacher. But they did not want to take away the satisfaction she felt at beginning to provide for herself. At the same time, they were worried about her living in the rather dangerous neighborhood where her job was located. They spoke with her about their concerns, and together they came up with a plan. Her parents would supplement her paycheck each month just enough to allow her to rent an apartment in a safer place. Her parents realized that this young woman's work was to become a great teacher, not to avoid getting mugged. Their financial support enhanced rather than subsidized her life because it allowed her to do her true work.

Thinking about work this way helps solve a riddle that besets many people within families with financial wealth, including members of the rising generation. If you have the means to do so, why not live on vacation? As one family member said to us (he was in his 40s and his family had sold their successful business a few years before), "When my kids ask me what I do, I say I'm retired. And now I realize that they have been born retired." He did not feel good about this situation. He felt he was depriving his children of an important experience, and that his own life-path had been cut short.

The reason is that vacations, or retirement, or relaxations in general—as fun as they are—are truly worthwhile because they provide a pause from work. When we work, we get tired. We need a break. But if you never work, then you really never enjoy a break. In such a situation, going from one vacation or fun activity to another can start to feel like drudgery. It is like a weekend that never ends. It becomes as boring as any dead-end job.

This is, then, another reason for the importance of work. If you do not work, it will be hard to enjoy your down time. But the interconnection between work and relaxation also points to one last important consideration. If relaxation is truly for the sake of work (because it helps us catch our breath), and if work puts others' needs or goods ahead of our own, then what about our own good? Is the world a giant hamster wheel in which we serve each other's good, take a break, and then start spinning round again? That too sounds like a recipe for eventual boredom.

This problem is all the more acute when meeting your own needs (earning your bread) is not part of your reason for working. The resolution of this problem has led thinkers, from antiquity to the present, to postulate a third state, beyond work and relaxation: the state of *ordered leisure*.[7] Leisure has a bad reputation today. The overwhelming praise of work makes leisure sound lazy. But, in truth, leisure is the opposite of laziness. Using your leisure well can be one of the greatest challenges of life amid wealth. Ordered leisure does not mean sitting around watching TV. It involves cultivating your abilities so as not only to benefit others (such as in work) but also to make yourself happier and your life more flourishing. Cultivating leisure means not only doing what is useful but also appreciating what is beautiful. It means not only figuring out what is practical but also marveling at what is true.

You know from reading thus far that we, as authors and as advisers, give much more importance to *human* capital than to *financial* capital. But this is the one place where we would grant *financial* capital's true utility. The possibility of ordered leisure—and not just the endless cycle of work and play—is, in our view, the highest and best justification for financial wealth. But it is hard to appreciate the high possibility of ordered leisure if you have not first come to appreciate the importance of work.

Relationships

Let us move now from Freud's "labor" to his "love." From ancient times to the present, relationships have been one of the foremost concerns for members of the rising generation. Two and a half millennia ago, Aristotle commented on the ease with which young people seek out and develop friendships.[8] And today, to *friend* and to *like* other people have become ubiquitous verbs.

The importance of relationships to the rising generation brings with it a crucial question: how can you choose wisely those friends or that partner with whom you want to journey through the next month, the next year, or possibly the rest of your life? Though most of us do not face the choice this clearly, it is a critical one. As one mother we knew observed: "I spent so much time worrying about which schools my children got into, I didn't realize then that the choice of whom they would marry was far more important." Let us make the most of her wisdom.

The contemporary world does not make it easy to do so. Today, relationships are often divided between two opposite poles. On the one hand are our supposed friends of self-interest: people from whom we expect to get some benefit, such as business associates or classmates. You may like such people; you may also do them favors. But the word *friend* here is pretty loose.

On the other hand, there is the ideal of romance, the one true love of your life. It is a beautiful dream, but it is hard to see how to find this wonderful person. These two poles play off each other. Dissatisfaction with always pursuing self-interest can make people dream of romance. And disappointment when the reality of romance does not live up to the ideal can make people figure that there is, in the end, nothing but looking out for number one. It is perhaps fitting that the current fad of likes and friend requests all take place within the context of a business (Facebook) devoted to advertising.

Still, the flourishing of social media within the largely asocial world of the Internet shows that the desire for connection lives strong. How, then, can you, members of the rising generation, pursue that desire wisely, especially within the context of wealth?

First, consider yourself. When have you been a true friend? Think about the friendships you have had, going back to childhood. Who have been your best friends? Review the interests or the activities that led to your becoming friends. Spend a moment to remember the actions that you took that established or reestablished your friendships over the years.

Next, think about your present circumstances. Who are your friends now? This may be a somewhat difficult question to answer. Do business associates or people you see only in classes count as friends? Do lovers? Spend a moment with these difficulties. In the case of friends with benefits, do those benefits make the other more of a friend—or less of one? Think about what these difficulties say about what friendship does (or does not) mean to you.

The difficulty of enumerating our friends is a natural and enduring one. The ancient Greek philosopher Socrates used to joke to his young companions that they could, on a moment's notice, tally up how many horses or dogs they had, but they had to scratch their heads and think about it if he asked them how many friends they had. And yet, he would point out, how much more valuable than a horse or a dog is a true friend![9] The same goes today. If you are financially literate, you may have at your fingertips how much money you have in the bank or in investment accounts. But do you know who your true friends are?

Now let us turn from the past and present to the future, for friends and other relations are not like money in the bank: they are dynamic, not static. They require cultivation. The question, then, is how to cultivate positive relationships. In doing so, we suggest keeping a few points in mind:

- Cultivate relationships with people who *affirm your strengths*. So many times, out of fear of being alone or the pressure to fit in, people choose friends who play on their weaknesses. A friend who affirms your best qualities can make you much stronger than you ever dreamed of being on your own. Nor is this a selfish choice. A truly positive relationship is greater than the sum of its parts. A friend who makes you stronger makes you a better friend, too. It is a virtuous circle.

- Cultivate relationships with people who *share your dreams*. This sounds like a simple point. If you are committed to philanthropy, for example, seek out friendships with people who share that commitment, and so on. But so many of us endure relationships where there is no shared dream simply because of inertia, complacency, or embarrassment. Staying in relationships that lack any sort of shared dream is like trying to pilot a ship in two different directions. A shared dream, in contrast, gives a powerful wind behind both your sails.

- Cultivate relationships with people who are *positive and forward focused*. No one enjoys negative naysayers. And yet, how often do many of us find ourselves spending our precious time with such people! The point here is not to drop a friend who is going through a tough time. Rather, it is to distinguish between someone who is negative because of his or her condition and someone who is negative as a state of being. A mother we know summed up this rule by saying, "Don't spend time with people who suck the energy out of the room." A friend of hers refined the point: "You mean, 'Don't spend time with people who suck.'" Though stated crudely, it is a memorable rule of thumb.

- Finally, cultivate relationships with *people who challenge you to be the best you can be.* Your friends do not need to be on your back all the time the way a football coach or piano teacher might. As we said, you want them to affirm you for who you are. But who you are also includes your potential, your ability to be more than who you are now. Achilles would not have been the hero he was without his friend Patroclus, nor would have King David without his friend Jonathan. The same goes for Augustus, the first true Roman emperor and his friend Marcus Agrippa; Abraham Lincoln and his friend Joshua Speed; and, on a humbler scale, your three co-authors vis-à-vis one another.

These rules of thumb do not encompass the whole of choosing wisely when it comes to relationships. Clearly, that work also involves being there for your friends when they need you, sticking through the tough times, and being willing to admit your mistakes. Relationships can be like bones: a break can sometimes make the healed relationship all the stronger. At the same time, honoring friendship sometimes means recognizing when a friendship has faded away, for whatever reasons, and that it is time to move on.

Financial wealth adds complexity to what is already a complex matter. So think first about how to choose relationships well simply as relationships. *Then* add the money to the equation. For example, if you have significant financial wealth, it is natural to wonder if someone who wishes to become your friend wants to because of who you are or because of the things you can buy. Likewise, being friends with someone with lesser means than you can lead to difficulties around spending money together on meals, drinks, vacations, and other adventures. Similarly, your friends with less could suspect that you may try to use your money to lead the pack and control their choices.

These are natural complexities. But if you keep in mind the points we listed earlier—to look for friends who affirm your strengths, who share your dreams, who are positive and forward focused, and who challenge you—you and your friends will be able, together, to resolve these dilemmas. There is an old saying that "there is no justice among friends." The saying obviously does not mean that friends should treat each other unjustly. Instead, it means that friends, unlike strangers or casual acquaintances, do not have to keep track of every favor they do or every favor they receive. Friends do not need to keep a balance sheet of assets and liabilities in some sort of friendship bank. That is why there is no hard-and-fast rule for managing friendships within the context of wealth. To switch metaphors, the key is to make sure you get the right people on the bus. If you do, then you will be able to navigate these dilemmas with little or no trouble. If you do not, then all the rules in the world will not help.

The work of navigating friendships reminds us of a young man we knew who found out in his late teens that he was going to receive significant wealth from his parents and grandparents. He had never thought much about relationships, though he was by nature a generous person. When he was in college, he started seriously dating a woman. He told her about his possible inheritance. After a few months of dating, he found that he had real reservations about the relationship—she was very negative about his family and various other people in his life—but he felt bad breaking it off since he took a rather traditional view of marrying someone with whom he had been intimate. He was also worried about being alone. He silenced his reservations in order, as he saw it, "to do the right thing." He endured an unhappy relationship and marriage for many years. When he finally decided to leave the relationship, he learned that his spouse had long seen him as a way for her to "never be poor."

Unsurprisingly, this young man told us after this experience that he came to believe that no relationship can ever work out, especially when money is involved. However, eventually he did meet someone who did affirm his strengths, with whom he shared dreams, who was positive and forward focused (in ways his former spouse never could be with him), and who challenged him to continue to grow. It took time and many conversations, but he and his new partner found that they could talk through and resolve money issues and other relationship issues that he could never imagine even raising, much less resolving, in his prior marriage.

This story points to the paramount place of relationships in life, and the paramount place of resilience in relationships. Money is important, but it is a secondary factor. If you reflect on the questions raised above and the practices we suggest, you will develop your own resilient relationships, and they will prove to be perhaps the greatest part of your true wealth.

Communication

Like work and relationships, communication is a big topic; it touches all of our relations with other people. In this section we want to focus in on the communication between you, as members of the rising generation, and your parents, grandparents, trustees or others who control the family's financial wealth. These are crucial relationships within which to find your voice.

This is a topic that we have been asked about countless times by members of rising generations and their parents. (We will use *parents* here as a stand-in for parents, grandparents, trustees, or anyone else in authority.) Each side would like to know: how do I start the conversation? What should I say? What should I not say? It can be so hard to talk with our closest family members about money. As one father we knew said, "I have no problem talking with my son about sex. But whenever I think about talking about money, I just start to choke." We suspect his son felt the same (perhaps about both topics!). It is a place where resilience can make all the difference.

First, it is important to recognize how normal this difficulty is. Do you know what your parents' income is? If you are working, do they know what your salary is? Do you know how much your best friends or your siblings make? Probably not. Money truly is the last taboo. The father who felt like choking when he attempted to bring up money with his son was experiencing a completely normal reaction. It would have been surprising if he found it easy to raise these topics with his son.

Given this difficulty, what can you, as a member of the rising generation, do to communicate effectively? Perhaps the most important thing is to evaluate realistically who your parents are. Sometimes people are so close to us that it is hard to see them. Other times, we know just who our parents are but we wish they were different. It is hard to wish that your father or mother would be more understanding, more communicative, or more open. But it is far better to accept your parents' limitations and plan accordingly than to bang your head against a reality that will not change.

For example, we knew a young man whose father had created an extremely successful retail business. This young man worked well in his father's company until it was sold for a significant sum. At that point the son was in his 30s, and he realized that he did not want to take a job in another company. He wanted to try to become a successful author. He had never really talked with his father about money before. He reflected on who his father was: generous, deeply loyal, but also proudly self-made and fairly controlling. With these realities in mind, the young man approached his father and told him about his dream. He explained that to take the time to write a marketable manuscript, he would need to leave work. He would therefore need some money to live on. His father gladly embraced his son's project and declared that he wanted to make a gift equivalent to his son's annual salary in order to give him two years to work on his book. It was a warm and happy conversation.

And because he had prepared himself beforehand, the son did not react when his father took many weeks to make the gift. Nor did he react when, several times in the months that followed, his father questioned his purchases of new clothes and a new car, asking how his son could afford such purchases. He knew that his father could not help making such observations, and he did not respond with anger or resentment. Because he did not react, his father did not press the issue. In the end, the son was able to write the manuscript, secure an agent, and publish his book, launching himself, with his father's generous help, in a new career.

In another case, a mother approached us because she was quite upset with her 20-something daughter. This mother liked to give her children checks for thousands of dollars as holiday gifts. But her daughter had told her that she did not believe in the holidays and did not want the gift. We spoke with both the mother and daughter and helped them hear each other. The daughter had found it hard to hear her mother's desire to benefit her. The daughter thought that her mother was just being controlling. In turn, the mother had found it hard to hear her daughter's desire to make it on her own. When each one truly listened to the other, they found that they actually agreed on many points regarding the commercialization of the holidays and the importance of human relations rather than money.

The main lesson here is that resilience has its place in communication and that the key to resilient communication is a realistic assessment of yourself and the person with whom you are communicating. The young man in our story knew that his father would value his taking on a new challenge. He also knew that his father simply could not make a gift with no strings attached. If you are thinking about talking with your parents about the family's finances, first get clear about the goal of your conversation. Is it to learn? To take some action? To offer your thoughts? To get their direction? Be clear about who they are and, based on their characters, how you think they will hear what you have to say. Then, listen and learn from what they say—not only from their words but how they say what they say. Finally, be prepared to observe yourself, so that you do not get pulled in emotionally and react in a way that will not help you achieve your goals.

Leaving Ithaca

After the nobles of Ithaca laughed him down, it would have been easy for Telemachus to slink away and shut up. He could have remained as a well-fed, well-clothed, quiet if resentful figure in his mother's house. His mother's suitors may have killed him eventually. But if he really did silence himself, perhaps they would have seen him as beneath contempt and would have left him to live out his days in modest luxury and peace.

But what a terrible life that would have been! Instead, Telemachus bounced back from this initial disappointment. True, he had some divine encouragement. But he also possessed a seed of resilience in his heart.

This chapter has been about taking leaps and bouncing back from the inevitable challenges of life. Recognizing the power of the black hole is important. Knowing yourself is crucial. But perhaps the greatest task—and maybe the most overlooked task—for rising generations in families with wealth is developing resilience. Resilience is core to individuation. Every time you take on a work assignment—every time you apprentice yourself, even to a crotchety, difficult boss—every time you reach a hand out to a possible friend—every time you make an attempt to understand and communicate with a parent—every one of these actions is an opportunity for you to build your resilience. Other skills or areas of knowledge (such as financial literacy) will allow you to do various things, accomplish tasks, and maybe even make money. But resilience will allow you to individuate, find your voice, avoid dependency and entitlement, and truly rise.

Question for Reflection

Pick one example each in your life of (1) true work, (2) a positive relationship, and (3) authentic communication. What makes each example distinctive?

Notes

1. Isolation can have its negative side and its positive side, too. Odysseus himself says about his homeland of Ithaca, perhaps thinking about Telemachus: "My home is on the peaked sea-mark of Ithaca . . . A rocky isle, but good for a boy's training;/I shall not see on earth a place more dear . . ." *Odyssey* IX, Robert Fitzgerald, trans. (New York, NY: FSG, 1961), 146.

2. For more on this point from an analytical but very practical perspective, see Judith Stern Peck, *Money and Meaning* (Hoboken, NJ: Wiley, 2007).

3. See Howard Gardner, Mihaly Cziskzentmihalyi, and William Damon, *Good Work* (New York, NY: Basic Books, 2002).

4. For strong statements of this view, see Scott Shane, *Born Entrepreneurs, Born Leaders: How Your Genes Affect Your Work Life* (New York, NY: Oxford University Press, 2010); and James L. Fisher and James V. Koch, *Born, Not Made: the Entrepreneurial Personality* (New York, NY: Praeger, 2008).

5. The best practices of family enterprises that have passed the test of time are the subject of a growing body of knowledge. For groundbreaking work in this field, see our colleague Dennis Jaffe's work, *Good Fortune: Building a Hundred Year Family Enterprise* (Boston, MA: Wise Counsel Research, 2013).

6. See Gardner, Cziskzentmihalyi, and Damon, 2002.

7. See Aristotle, *Nicomachean Ethics*, Joseph Sachs, trans. (Newburyport, MA: Focus Press, 2002), Book X, chapter 7; Thomas Aquinas, *Commentary on the Metaphysics,* John P. Rowan, trans. (New York: Dumb Ox Books, 1995), I.t.lect. 3; and Josef Pieper, *Leisure: the Basis of Culture* (New York, NY: Ignatius Press, 2009).

8. See Aristotle, *op. cit.*, Books VIII and IX.

9. See Xenophon, *Memorabilia of Socrates*, Amy Bonnette, trans. (Ithaca, NY: Cornell University Press, 2001), Book I.

Chapter 5

The Middle Passage

The Island of the Lotus-Eaters

Early in Odysseus's attempt to return home from Troy, he and
his crew land on an island unknown to them. Unaware of any
danger, Odysseus sends three of his men ashore to see if it is
inhabited. When they do not return, he goes after them and finds
them among a strange race of human beings: the Lotus-Eaters.
These people do not threaten or harm Odysseus and his men.
Instead, they simply offer them the sweet Lotus flower to eat.
Anyone who does eat immediately forgets all about his journey
home, content to spend his whole life grazing on the flower.

Odysseus drives his men who have already eaten back to their
ships; they wail and cry, but he forces them aboard. He then
orders the rest of his crew to start rowing, warning them of the

danger of eating the Lotus. They escape. Little do they know that they sail next to the island of the Cyclops.

Though brief, the story of the island of the Lotus-Eaters is beguiling. The flower does represent a threat to Odysseus and his companions. It is not the typical threat they face, of physical violence or winds or waves. In a certain sense, it is a more profound danger. The flower strikes at the root of their desire to strive and to struggle. It eliminates their wish to return home. It causes them to forget what really matters. It turns them from men into a sort of docile, grazing animal or even into a kind of plant, content to live out their lives rooted to that spot.

At the same time, the Lotus represents a sort of promise. Odysseus and his men have faced 10 years of war. Just prior to landing at the island of the Lotus-Eaters they fled an island where they fought a pitched battle and lost many of their comrades. They are, unknowingly, sailing on to further violence and disasters. The Lotus promises calm and peace, a sort of anesthetized, twilight sleep. It is soothing and pleasant. It makes life simple. Who has not dreamed at some point of leaving the complications of human life behind? The Lotus fulfills that dream. The men who have eaten it weep upon being dragged away: even a few bites are that good.

The land of wealth resembles the island of the Lotus-Eaters. Whether we are living there or are on the outside looking in, most people recognize the beguiling combination of attraction and danger that financial wealth promises. And most of us are like those three members of Odysseus's crew: eager to eat the flower and despondent if it is taken away.

The attraction and the danger are all the greater if you have grown up on the island. The allure of the flower is all around you. It may be all that you have ever known and your sole diet. How hard is it to remember what really matters, to remember your journey, if every memory brings you home to the Lotus!

The previous chapters are meant to help you begin to break the flower's spell. They offer lessons and practices to help you rise, not as a plant but as a person. In this chapter, we want to extend this work to members of the rising generation who have spent an even longer time amid the flowers. We mean members of the rising generation who have passed their 20s and 30s and may be in their 40s, 50s, or even 60s. Rising in this stage of life involves many of the challenges that we have discussed in the previous four chapters. But it also involves challenges specific to this stage. As the story of the *Odyssey* suggests, the longer you live among the Lotus, the harder it is to break free. But it can be done. We hope that this chapter helps members of the rising generation who are in midlife, as well as instructs younger rising generation family members so that they can prepare for or even prevent the dangers that may lie ahead.

The Middle Passage

The middle passage is a term we use, following psychologist James Hollis, to describe the journey through midlife.[1] As Erik Erikson observed, midlife can be seen as a struggle between generativity and stagnation: which will prevail? Our bodies and maybe even our minds generally begin to slow down. Aspirations or hopes for education or career may have been disappointed or at least not turned out as we expected. We have, at this point in life, usually lived through significant relationships that did not work out. The sense of futurity that is so important to rising (recall Chapter 2) may begin to fade in the face of the mortality of our parents, friends, and perhaps even ourselves. The impact of all these factors causes for some people a midlife crisis, in which they dramatically break with past careers, relationships, or patterns of behavior. For others, these factors give rise to a long period of reassessment, reflection, and reprioritization. Whether dramatic or subtle, all these changes are part of the middle passage. The result of the struggle between generativity and stagnation will determine whether, in the final stage of life, we rise into integrity or fall into despair.

Growing up as a member of the rising generation within a family of wealth adds complications to this already complicated passage. To illustrate, consider the case of a man we knew whom we will call Frank. Frank was about 50, the oldest of his four siblings. Their parents had run a successful transportation company, which they sold for several million dollars when Frank was in his mid-30s. Frank, his three brothers, and his one sister had all worked in the company. When we met Frank, he was working as head of his family's private foundation, but he admitted that he did not have much to do. He attended conferences, visited charitable organizations, and made the rounds of pleasant lunches every quarter or so at the invitation of the foundation's investment managers, accountants, or lawyers. One of his brothers played a similar role as head of the family's family office (which really just involved a part-time bookkeeper). Another brother was the family's estate manager, in charge of keeping the various homes maintained. His third brother was supervisor of some commercial properties the family still owned. (He delegated the actual supervision to a real estate management company he hired.) And Frank's sister organized semiannual family meetings and retreats (i.e., the family vacations). Each of the siblings received a modest stipend for his or her work. All these jobs were as undemanding as Frank's.

When we met him, Frank was dissatisfied. He was wondering, "Is this all there is to life?" He did not mind his role at the foundation, but it was not his calling. He also recognized that neither he nor his siblings had truly chosen their work. Their father, who in his late 80s was still very much alive and in charge, had assigned these roles to them. None of them had resisted. As Frank said, "We all went with the flow, and before we knew it we had been living this way for years." As a result, although Frank felt dissatisfied, he had a hard time imagining any other path. He was firmly planted among the Lotus flowers.

A Forceful Hand

One lesson the story of the *Odyssey* teaches is that you do not typically leave the island of the Lotus-Eaters on your own. The three sailors who had eaten the flower required the strenuous efforts of Odysseus and their companions to remove them—by force—from the island.

The situation is similar for members of the rising generation who find themselves in the middle passage amid financial wealth. As with most challenges in life, the first step in addressing it is becoming aware that you have a problem. Too many people do not even reach that point. Financial wealth, like the Lotus flower, can cause forgetfulness: forgetfulness of what life is like without the money, forgetfulness of why work is important, forgetfulness of what authentic relationships are like, and forgetfulness of one's own dreams or the very possibility of having dreams.

Some people, like Frank, do awaken to the awareness that something is not right. Sometimes the expression of that awareness takes the form of complaining about boredom. A life of doing nothing—even if, in the best case, that "nothing" takes the form of lots of conscientious meetings and lunches—can be as boring as a life beside an assembly line. People without financial wealth may be incredulous at hearing wealthy 40- or 50-somethings complain about being bored. Yet that incredulity does not make the boredom any less stifling or real.

Boredom or self-reflection helps some people in the middle passage awaken to the dangers that the founder's dream and its materialization into financial wealth pose to rising. But for many others, it takes a crisis. Frank awoke to his question, "Is this all there is to life?" when he was confronted with his parents' old age and disability and his mother's death. One woman we know awoke to the problem when her husband of 15 years asked her for a divorce. She had never thought seriously about her finances, her career path, or her dreams. Suddenly, she was faced with a threat to her assets and the possibility that she might no longer have the choice of just flowing through life. Another woman of our acquaintance awoke when her father sold the family business, at which she had worked for years. The sale did not deprive her of a livelihood: she became the beneficiary of a generous trust. But it did take from her a title and sense of identity that had allowed her to justify, at least in her own mind, her good fortune. Receiving a trust distribution each month felt a lot different than earning a paycheck.

Still, even when awake to the problem, breaking old patterns usually requires a helping hand—sometimes a forceful one. In this situation, the isolation that wealth brings with it can strongly threaten wealth holders' well-being. (*Isolation* comes from the Latin word for *island*.) Just as with the Lotus-Eaters ensconced on their island, the isolation that wealth brings can make it all the less likely that a helping hand will find you.

So where can you find it? The first place to look is within your family. For example, if you have siblings who are also in the middle passage of life, can you help one another? Sibling relationships are among the closest—and the most fraught. Many grown siblings love each other but make sure to keep a respectful distance from one another's personal space. This respect is prudent, but there are times when it can be counter-productive. If you and your siblings grew up on the island of the Lotus-Eaters, then you know each other's situation well. You know the temptations and the disappointments of that life. If you are in your 30s, 40s, or beyond, then the rivalries and hurt of childhood or teenage years have likely cooled or at least receded. It is precisely as mature adults that you can pose those hard questions to each other: "Is this all there is? Could there be something more? What would that something more look like?" You can also encourage each other in the hard work of knowing yourselves, building resilience, and starting to rise, even in the middle passage. Indeed, this could be one of the most powerful acts of love that you as a sibling can show to your brothers or sisters.

Cousins can play a similar role, though it may be harder, since the relationship is typically not as close. Still, that emotional distance may, in some cases, make it easier for mature cousins to make each other aware of the big questions, since they are not burdened with sibling rivalry or old patterns of birth-order behavior. However, in many families, we have seen cousins help each other inadvertently: it is the failure, addiction, or disgrace of a cousin that causes others in the family to look at their own lives and to start on the road to making a change. We would not wish anyone to see his or her cousin fail. But it is striking that these negative examples can work some powerful good—perhaps even more good than seeing your cousins succeed. Maybe seeing the effect of the flower on their shipmates helped deter some of the rest of Odysseus's crew from running with open arms into the fields of Lotus?

Another challenge for both siblings and cousins in the middle passage is geographic dispersion. It is not uncommon for wealth to enable adult family members to go their own ways, sometimes spreading out across a continent or the world. While such dispersion is not unusual, it does make it hard to be aware of one another's condition, to offer your siblings or cousins help, and to encourage each other in this journey. If this dispersion is the case in your family, then look for the opportunities to connect, or reconnect, and learn about how your siblings or cousins are doing. Perhaps these opportunities are traditional holidays, or birthdays, or anniversaries of various sorts. Perhaps you could be the one to suggest a family reunion or a family meeting or retreat. Whatever the occasion, consider getting together those family members in the middle passage of life. Set aside some time simply to update each other on how your lives are going. Do not expect to solve your problems or resolve crises in such a gathering. The greatest outcome may be to have a better sense of each other, your current paths and struggles, and to create a basis for one-on-one conversations as appropriate.

But if that helping hand is not likely to come from within your family, do not lose hope. Sometimes it is possible to find organizations that provide a forum to discuss the benefits and the dangers that financial wealth poses to healthy development. For example, we lead a program, Wise Counsel Research Seminars, to gather wealth holders across the country in workshops to discuss such matters as work, relationships, communication, and parenting. After several meetings, members of these workshops develop a sense of community and find ways to connect and help each other even outside the seminar setting. Whatever the venue, consider such groups with a view toward such questions as:

- If I spend my time—my most precious resource—on membership in this group, will it help me in my journey through the middle passage?
- Will being part of this group help move me away from the island of the Lotus-Eaters? Or will going to these meetings amount to yet another serving of flowers?

The answers to these questions depend very much on the composition of the group, its mission, and the thoughtfulness and courage of its leaders. There is nothing easier than serving Lotuses to Lotus-Eaters, which in this context amounts to stroking the egos and nursing the insecurities of the wealthy. It is quite a different thing to follow Odysseus's lead and in a loving but firm, empathic but determined way, to give people the courage to break free from past patterns of behavior. Such leaders and such groups are rare. When you find one, give it your all and you will not be disappointed.

Self-Advocacy

The Odyssey gives the impression that the island of the Lotus-Eaters is a rather quiet place. The inhabitants spend their time grazing on flowers, after all. This is also a quality that we have observed among many members of the rising generation who have come to the middle passage of life amid financial wealth: silence pervades.

As we noted in the Introduction and Chapter 1, this silence is unsurprising. In many families with financial wealth, the only voice that counts belongs to the founder or founders. They have materialized their great dream into money. They have spoken forth or set down "the family's" values. They may have enunciated a mission for the family and their future descendants. They very likely are the ones who have established trusts and other structures that map out what assets or income their descendants will get, at what points in life, and even in exchange for what sorts of behavior. Their word is law: the dictates of a new Ozymandias. It is no wonder that this dynamic instills silence in their recipients. All is said.

It is all the more crucial, then, for members of the rising generation in the middle passage to reclaim or discover their voices. Sometimes, as we mentioned earlier, this voice takes the form of complaints, such as complaining about boredom. It may express complaints about living a life in which every major decision seems to have been mapped out by your parents or grandparents. Such complaints are something: they are not silence. The first thing Odysseus's men did when he dragged them from the Lotus-Eaters was to cry. The reaction is a normal one.

In many other cases, the voice of people in the middle passage first expresses itself in regret or guilt. It is not generally acknowledged, but it is hard to be a recipient. Most people see recipients as passive, maybe as undeserving, and certainly as less impressive than the founders who make the financial wealth that the others receive. Many recipients view themselves this way, too. The result often is that you may feel guilty at receiving: as a woman at one of our presentations asked, "Why have I been given all this and not others? What have I done to deserve this fortune?" You may also feel regret at choices or experiences that you did not have precisely because you did not have to work for your livelihood or your assets. This is not being a poor little rich girl (or boy). It is being human.

Expressing these complaints, regrets, or feelings of guilt is a way to begin to find your voice. It can help to have a group of sympathetic friends or siblings or cousins to share these words with. It is also important to take the steps we describe in Chapter 3. Use your complaints, regrets, or guilt not as a stopping point but as a beginning. Use them to lead to the questions, "Who am I? What are my dreams? What are the hurdles within me that have kept me from moving forward? What are the hurdles external to me that have gotten in my way?"

Once you have started down this path to self-knowledge, with a helping hand from others, it is also important to use your voice to advocate for yourself. Doing so is perhaps the greatest challenge for someone in the middle passage of life who has become used to being a recipient and being controlled by whomever is handing out the Lotus flowers. Maybe that person is a parent. Maybe he or she is a trustee. Whoever it is, use your voice to advocate for yourself to that authority.

For example, Frank, whom we described earlier, was moved by his self-reflection to seek out others with whom to talk. He joined one of our seminars, which was composed of wealth holders who were of a similar age and facing similar questions. As a result of those sessions, he started a program to educate himself in art history, a field that he had always wanted to study but never had the courage to do so. He used his position in the foundation to work more closely with museums and other arts groups. He also started convening conversations with his four siblings to talk about their respective life paths. He worked with us individually over several sessions to help advance his own thinking and doing.

As a result of these meetings, and with the help of one of us as a facilitator, Frank and his siblings eventually asked their father to join one of their meetings. They expressed to him a strong desire to remain connected as a family. But they also explained that they thought many of the roles that he had assigned to them could be handled more effectively and efficiently by nonfamily experts. They recognized that their dad had the ultimate say over who provided those services. And they knew that not performing those services themselves would involve a loss of some income. But they were willing to forgo that income in order to have the freedom to pursue their own dreams.

Once their father recognized that their intention was not to abandon the family (and him), he found their proposal attractive. He respected their resolve to seek their own paths and he expressed a desire to help them do so, if he could. He was particularly impressed by their concern that if they did not do this work for themselves, they could be setting a destructive example for their children, his grandchildren. As much as he enjoyed keeping his children close, within his kingdom, he did not want to see his desires harm his grandchildren.

Frank's example shows that even when things go quite smoothly, finding your voice in the middle passage of life is no easy task. It takes many steps and many people's involvement and support. But it can be done.

Ownership

Our focus thus far has been in helping members of the rising generation in the middle passage of life find your voice. This may be a collective effort, involving many people's help. But, ultimately, it is your voice that you need to discover.

This point—that the voice you want to find is your own—leads directly to a topic of great importance to the rising generation generally but especially to rising generation members in the middle passage, the topic of ownership. It is your *own* voice, after all, that we have just been discussing, not someone else's. And yet this seemingly simple point is exactly the one that can become obscured within families with financial wealth. The unnatural, legal relationships of trusts or business entities; the family name and all it entails; the expectations for togetherness, even in vacations or choice of residences—all these complications can cause you to forget who you are and where the boundaries of your own voice or your own life lie.[2]

Part of the challenge, then, is to become a great owner—of your property, your time, your talents, and yourself. But what if you have been told that you do not own much at all? "Your" supposed assets may be tied up in trusts, of which you are only the beneficial owner. A trustee—perhaps a family member or professional adviser, perhaps a corporation—may be the legal owner. The legal owner may also have the power to decide how and when you benefit from "your" property. What if your parents own your house or supply the money to allow you to purchase a home, or if they or other family members own the property that allows you to go to school, work, or otherwise pursue "your" dreams?

The challenge captured in these questions has only become greater over time, as family financial assets flow into trusts. In *The Cycle of the Gift*, we describe what we call a *trust wave* that by the second or third generation tends to carry more than 90 percent of a family's financial wealth into trust. The problem with this trust wave is not legal or financial. Legal or financial considerations are, after all, usually the reasons that lead to the trust wave. Rather, the problem is human. In family after family that we have seen, members of the rising generation feel separated from important choices in their lives by the unnatural relationship of a trust. They find themselves dependents of trustees over whose selection they may have little or no control. If you are in such an unnatural relationship, it may cause you to feel like an infant well into your late middle age.

It is precisely because of these complexities that taking ownership is a crucial challenge for rising generations, especially for those members in the middle passage of life. The first step in facing that challenge is to clarify what you do and do not own and in what ways you do or do not own these things. It is easier to say than to do. For example, we knew a young woman who had grown up with wealth and who had long heard about various trusts or other entities of which she was a beneficiary. She never thought much about these structures until, in the midst of an unhappy marriage, she decided to get a divorce. Suddenly, and in a highly adversarial environment, she was faced with such questions as, "Is this my property? Marital property? Family property?" Her parents were clear: it was all family property, not to be touched by the divorce. Her husband was clear: it was all marital property, subject to division. She was at a loss. The divorce prompted very important work for her. A critical part of the legal settlement depended on her own process of getting clear about what she considered her own, what she needed to live on, and what she was willing to part with.

An old saying holds that "we all come into the world with nothing, and we leave with nothing." Members of the rising generation within a family with wealth may beg to differ, at least with the first part. You may have been born with quite a lot, at least to your name. The task, then, is to integrate that property into your life. That work is not just a matter of making an inventory or transferring title. It is not something that can be done for you by a trustee or by the person who made the money. It requires that you become clear both about what you have, as we just said, and then about what you want this property to do for you.

This step is part of a larger piece of work: deconstructing the unnatural trust relationships and then constructing more natural, more human relationships in their place. That deconstruction starts with recognizing the trust wave as a problem and the need to own your own life. It is furthered by learning what is set in stone and what is changeable within the trusts that you are dealing with. The construction starts by getting clear about what you want the trust property to do for you. And it is furthered by seeking to present yourself as a human being, not just as a "bene," to a trustee or trust officer who is also a human being, not just a fiduciary or an institution. This last task is a critical example of self-advocacy.[3]

Leadership

This is the place to speak briefly about a related topic: leadership. Leadership is a core topic in discussions of family enterprise. There are centers for family enterprise leadership at business schools or within consulting companies. Sometimes it seems as though everyone involved in family business or family wealth is on the lookout for leaders or on the path of developing leadership.

As important as leadership is, the demand to be a leader can become just another variant of the black hole or the Lotus flower. In family after family, we see members of the rising generation thrust too early into positions such as that of trustee of family members' trusts or director of family companies or philanthropies. These positions are important. But devoting yourself to them too soon may stymie your own natural development. As Frank saw in his role as head of his family's foundation, his father's demand that he "lead" was a sort of snare.

For these reasons, if you want to be a leader, consider the first task of leadership to be leading your own life. As we saw in Chapter 4, Telemachus thought that he could lead just because he was Odysseus's son. The nobles of Ithaca soon put him in his place. Leaving his kingdom and pursuing his own path were the prerequisites to his returning as a true leader.

For a more contemporary example, we are reminded of a young man we knew who grew up with a mother and several younger sisters. Thanks to traditional gender biases and his own abilities, his mother and his sisters looked to him, even at a relatively young age, to lead them in the management of their wealth and philanthropies. At first, he took on this task gladly. He was proud of his leadership. But, over time, he realized that his mother and sisters had skills that he did not possess. His supposed leadership was keeping their skills from being fully utilized. Also, his role as leader was keeping him from pursuing his own dreams. He began to feel burdened and even to resent his positions. He turned to friends and then to us, as advisers to his family, for help. After long reflection and discussion, he decided to make a plan to transition many of his roles to other family members or advisers. He discussed these steps with each of his family members, and, once they understood his motivation, they gladly supported his change.

This example further justifies the importance of self-advocacy for members of the rising generation, particularly members in the middle passage of life. It also underscores the importance of knowing when it would help to seek counsel. It can be very difficult to advocate for yourself or to ask for help. Your inclination may be to take care of others, and self-advocacy involves speaking up for yourself, sometimes forcefully. Still, if done thoughtfully and respectfully, it promotes productive change. It is a critical part of the leadership of leading your own life. And that is our fundamental work.

Parenting in the Middle Passage

Members of the rising generation who find themselves in the middle passage of life face one other challenge that is different from those faced by younger rising generation members: they are often parenting a new, rising generation of their own. To do this work well can be one of the most rewarding and most challenging endeavors in life.

The foundation for good parenting is the work we describe above and in Chapters 3 and 4, namely, taking ownership and leadership over your own life, being clear about your own dreams, developing your resilience, and pursuing those dreams to the best of your own abilities. Parents who feel good about their lives naturally start in a better position to help their children grow. In particular, if you know yourself and your dreams, you are less likely to project your hopes or disappointments onto your children.

The next step is, of course, to be clear about who your children are. Even within the same family, there can be amazing variety among children. Seeing your children for who they are is the basis for nurturing each of them.

We discuss each of these two steps more fully in Chapters 1 and 2 of *Cycle of the Gift*.[4] In addition to these steps, there are several other practices that we have found help members of rising generations raise a new, rising generation of children.

First, spend a moment reflecting on your own *younger self* as a member of a rising generation. What can you learn from your experience that would help you help your children? What did your parents do that helped you rise—in terms of rules, practices, or communication? What did they do that stymied your rising?

The point of this exercise is to learn from your experience but, even more importantly, to develop empathy for your own children and their experience as members of a rising generation.

Second, whether from your own experience or that of people you know, consider the importance of *space or openness* for your children versus structure. Most parents err on the side of structuring their children's lives. Financial wealth can greatly exacerbate this tendency. By freeing parents up from the need to work for others, it can leave them hovering about their children all day. It also gives them the resources to hire nannies, sitters, tutors, and teachers and to enroll their children in camps, after-school programs, lessons, and so forth. None of these people or practices is bad in itself. But openness or space is essential to children's development. Children need openness to explore the world around them. They also need space to try out their own abilities and so to learn about themselves. Imagine what would happen if you hired a servant to carry your son from place to place, so that he never had to sully his feet by touching the ground. You would end up with an adult child who could not walk on his own![5] Children cannot become free if they never have to practice freedom. And freedom is crucial to learning to rise.

This point connects closely to a third one: ask yourself what you can do to promote your children's *learning or training*. By learning we mean not their formal education, which they receive in school. We have in mind learning about themselves through such experiences as work. Most children from age eight or so onward have a desire to make things, to build things, and even to sell their products and engage in grown-up work. Encourage such activities—and do not try to structure them. Let your children learn about themselves by facing the challenge of making or doing something that meets the needs of others. As a related point, we caution you from being too eager to send your teens or 20-somethings to camps or programs designed to teach them about finances. Take yourself to such a program first: the content is probably more applicable to someone in the middle passage of life, someone who is trying to take ownership over his or her life, than someone just starting out. Your children's task is to learn about themselves, not about money that they may access only far off in the future.

Finally, if there is one thing that we have repeatedly heard from family members in the middle passage of life, it is the importance of *failure*. When we are raising our children, most of us seek to insulate them from any failure. After all, no one enjoys seeing his or her children in pain. But when you reflect upon your own life, what stand out as the moments when you learned the most valuable lessons? Were they the moments you won the prize? Or, more likely, were they the moments when you fell short, failed, and had to correct course? Apply that same insight to your parenting. If you never let your children take risks, they will never learn how to evaluate risks. They may become overly risk averse, or, conversely, they may take large risks without being aware of the danger. Likewise, if you never let them fail, they will never learn how to learn from challenges or disappointments. When a disappointment or failure comes along, as they eventually always do, it will be more likely to knock them completely off course. You will have deprived your children of the ability to develop their own resilience, which, as we saw in Chapter 4, is the key quality for individuation and rising.

Questions for Rising on Your Own

We began this chapter with the observation that people do not tend to leave the island of the Lotus-Eaters on their own. A helping hand is necessary. But what do you do if you are a member of the rising generation in the middle passage of life and you find yourself within a family in which there are simply no examples of a successful rise, no individuals to whom you can look for that helping hand?

Our first reaction to this situation has to be one of compassion. It is an extremely difficult place to be. But it is not unheard of. Some families we know have lived for generations amid the Lotus flowers in a state of twilight sleep. They may preserve some vague memories of individuals who found success in life. But when they look around at the people now living or living in the most recent past, they see only contented grazers, with perhaps a bit of indigestion here or there.

If you find yourself in this situation, with no one else in your present or prior generation to look to as an example of a successful rise, what can you do? As hard as it is, start by confronting yourself. To do so, here is a modified version of a series of questions that Jay Hughes presented in Chapter 13 of the revised version of his first book, *Family Wealth*.[6] These questions were designed to be asked by an independent adviser or counselor, whose job it is to evaluate the human capital of members of the rising generation of a family. But they can be adapted for the use of members of the rising generation themselves. In particular, they are best used by members in the middle passage of life, when you have some extended experience of living to reflect upon.

Ask yourself:

1. In what ways am I free? In what ways am I a dependent?
2. How self-aware am I—of my feelings? My abilities? My possibilities?
3. Have I sought to know my calling, not just my work or career, but my calling? If so, am I pursuing this calling? If I am not, why not?
4. Do I have a mentor? Have I ever had a mentor? If not, do I have the skills and knowledge to find a mentor? (On this point, please see the Conclusion to the current book.)

5. Have I ever humbled myself in order to serve as an apprentice and to learn what I need to know to pursue my calling? Have I had the experience of mastering a knowledge or skill important to me?
6. Do I have friends? Who are my friends? Who am I to each of them?
7. Can I express love? To whom have I done so?
8. Can I express compassion? Have I done so to myself? To others?
9. Can I express gratitude? When have I done so? How has it been received?
10. Do I feel joy now? Have I felt joy before? When?
11. Have I ever taken an active role in civil society or my community? Have I given to others? What did I give?
12. In which of these areas do I feel competent? In which of them do I feel I can grow?

These are not easy questions for anyone to answer. They may feel especially difficult to respond to if you find yourself in the middle passage of life feeling unfree and dependent and without much joy. But they are the sort of questions that helped Frank, for example, move from boredom and dissatisfaction to active engagement in recharting his life's path. They can provide some spark, some impetus to movement, even when you look around and see only grazing rather than rising. For, after all, true rising always comes from within. And it is never too late.

Reflective Exercise

Pick 1 of the 12 questions listed above and write out your thoughts in response to it. Let it sit for a day and then revisit what you wrote. Has your response changed at all? Over the next few months, try doing the same each week for the other 11 questions.

Notes

1. See James Hollis, *The Middle Passage: From Misery to Meaning at Midlife* (New York, NY: Inner City Books, 1993), and *Finding Meaning in the Second Half of Life* (New York, NY: Gotham Books, 2006).

2. We would recommend once more that you consider the work of our colleague Thayer Willis, who discusses the challenges of "deconstructing" "unnatural" relationships in *Beyond Gold: True Wealth for Inheritors* (Portland, OR: New Concord Press, 2012).

3. For the process of deconstructing unnatural relationships, we would refer the reader here once more to the excellent questions contained in Thayer Willis's *Beyond Gold* (see note 2) as well as the wonderful stories contained in Hartley Goldstone and Kathy Wiseman's *TrustWorthy: New Angles on Trusts from Beneficiaries and Trustees* (Denver, CO: Navigating the Trustscape, LLC, 2012).

4. For more on parenting within the context of affluence, see also Ellen Perry, *A Wealth of Possibilities: Navigating Family, Money, and Legacy* (Washington, DC: Egremont Press, 2012); Jennifer Senior, *All Joy and No Fun: The Paradox of Modern Parenthood* (New York, NY: Ecco Press, 2014); and Lee Hausner, *Children of Paradise* (Los Angeles, CA: Tarcher, 1990).

5. This is one of those places where true life is stranger than anything we as authors can imagine. For centuries, in China it was considered the height of fashion and a sign of affluence to bind women's feet to three inches in length. As a result, these women could barely walk and so had to be carried from place to place, demonstrating their wealth by their incapacity. In a further odd twist, connecting this practice to the theme of our chapter, the bound feet were referred to as "Lotus feet."

6. James E. Hughes, *Family Wealth: Keeping It in the Family* (New York, NY: Bloomberg, 2004), 133–136.

Conclusion

Another Well-Known Family

The Odyssey is a complicated poem. We have focused on the main storyline: Odysseus's wanderings, Telemachus's search for his father and his growth as a young man, and their successful return—as father and son—to reclaim their home. Naturally, we have left out many of the twists and turns in Homer's epic.

But here, in our conclusion, we want to single out a minor chord in *The Odyssey*'s symphony. Throughout *The Odyssey*, we hear mentions of one other family, of another Greek hero who went to Troy and who had a difficult homecoming. This family—the family of the Greek leader Agamemnon—is the shadow of the family of Odysseus.

At the very beginning of *The Odyssey*, the gods on high Olympus discuss Agamemnon's fate. He led the Greeks to Troy. (The gods do not mention it, but we know from other stories that, upon his launch, Agamemnon sacrificed his daughter, Iphigenia, in order to win the gods' favor for his expedition.) After 10 years besieging and then destroying Troy, he left with the main army and sailed home. But in the meantime, his wife, Clytemnestra, had taken up with another lord, Aegisthus. When Clytemnestra and Aegisthus heard that Agamemnon was returning, they prepared him a feast, pretended that all was well, and once Agamemnon had begun to eat and drink and let down his guard, they slaughtered him at his table.

The troubles did not end there. Agamemnon's son, Orestes, a hero in his own right, heard what his mother and her lover had done. He, too, returned home, caught them off guard, and slew them both. In punishment for killing his mother, the gods sent the Furies to hound Orestes across the whole of Greece.

Odysseus learns of Agamemnon's fate in the middle of *The Odyssey*, when he visits the underworld and speaks with Agamemnon's ghost. At the end of the entire poem, the spirits of the dead suitors also meet Agamemnon in the underworld. From beginning to end, the story of Agamemnon flits darkly about *The Odyssey*.

Agamemnon's story reminds us how wrong things can go. Penelope could have betrayed Odysseus. Odysseus could have returned home to a bloody reception. Telemachus could have slain his mother and ended up a fugitive. That matters turn out so well for Odysseus and his family seems miraculous in comparison.

Horror stories are commonplace in the land of wealth, too. How many of you have heard family members say that they do not want you or your siblings to end up as the latest bad boy or bad girl of Hollywood fame? How many of you know of an uncle, or an aunt, or an entire branch of your family that people will not discuss? These stories act like Agamemnon's ghost: haunting the present with tales from the past that instill fear about the future.

Agamemnon's ghost also highlights something that we touched upon in the Introduction: failure is normative. All families eventually dissolve. Financial wealth does slip away. Family life is difficult. "It's complicated," as people so often say. To acknowledge these realities is the first step in dealing with them thoughtfully.

But the comparison of Agamemnon with Odysseus reminds us that, despite failure's widespread presence, it is not the only possible outcome, right here, right now. Clytemnestra made one choice; Penelope made another. The same goes for Odysseus and Agamemnon, Orestes and Telemachus. Your family has choices. You have choices.

The interplay between the reality of failure and the possibility of choice is what makes rising within a family with financial wealth so difficult. In a moment we will recapitulate some of the lessons or principles that we shared in the chapters of this book. These lessons or principles may not all speak to you at this moment in your life or in your family's life. So much depends on the particulars: who you are, who your family is, and what you can do. The fact patterns of Odysseus' family situation and Agamemnon's family situation were not exactly the same, but they were pretty close. Yet similar facts led to remarkably different outcomes. Much of the work of attaining success as a member of the rising generation by finding your voice involves not only knowing the principles and lessons but also reflecting on the particulars of your situation and applying those principles and lessons accordingly. That is why we have encouraged your personal reflection throughout this work. It is also why we remind you here once more of your most important asset: your freedom to choose.

Our Journey Thus Far

Throughout this book, we have encouraged you to think of yourself as a member not of the next generation, nor of the second or third generation but rather of the *rising* generation. This linguistic shift is part of a larger reorientation: away from thinking about yourself just with respect to your family's financial wealth or only with respect to the creator of that financial wealth's amazing dream.

This reorientation reflects a surprising fact. Financial wealth is a massive materialization of something spiritual. That something spiritual is the founder's dream. An entrepreneur or other leader's drive, vision, and creativity are all expressions of human capital. When they take material form in great financial wealth, the transformation can seem almost miraculous.

But that materialization of human capital can in turn become a black hole. In family after family, we have seen it absorb all the attention, aspirations, and energies of other family members. How it does so takes many forms. It can control their lives, offering them no realm for choice and growth. It can dwarf their dreams, making them think they can never measure up. It can burden them with guilt. It can feed them the Lotus flower, so that they fall into a waking sleep. Whatever the way that the black hole operates, the result is the same: the family's human capital diminishes and disappears. The financial wealth eventually follows.

The response to that danger is to focus, with all your heart and mind, on the preservation and development of your human capital. Learning about financial capital—stocks, bonds, and the like—has its place. So, too, does becoming conversant with the legal structures that give shape to family financial wealth. But the primary task, here and now, is to learn about and become conversant with yourself, your abilities, and your dreams. That task involves getting clear about your abilities, your beliefs, and the internal and external hurdles you may face. It involves facing the possible limitations of your parents' abilities to parent you. It involves understanding the demographic opportunities—and baggage—that you have been born with. Reflecting on all these aspects of your identity as a member of the rising generation is the start.

This self-knowledge then provides the basis for development of your skills and particularly your capacity for resilience—the capacity to meet challenges in life and to bounce back rather than to crumble. One crucial way we saw that you can develop this resilience is through work: not just getting paid or holding a title but dedicating yourself to an activity you feel passionate about, humbling yourself through a period of apprenticeship, and truly focusing on others' good. Relationships are another area in which you can practice the development of resilience. Seek out relationships with others who affirm your strengths, who share your dreams, who keep you positive and focused forward, and who challenge you to be even better than you are. Finally, communication is an arena for developing resilience. Look for the serious conversations and people who will have serious conversations with you. Use these opportunities to understand the person you are speaking with. Prepare yourself by being clear about your goals in the discussion. This attitude and preparation will help you listen and learn and not react.

All of this self-reflection and these practices support the ultimate goal for you as a member of the rising generation: to become your own person, to individuate. This individuation takes place against the backdrop of your family of origin. It also takes place against the backdrop of your family's financial wealth. The goal of individuation is to remain connected with your family and its identity but, while doing so, to be yourself. Individuation is the answer to dependency or to entitlement. It is at the heart of rising. It is your path to liberation as it gives you voice.

Individuation is what is lost within the gravitational pull of the black hole. It is also what makes the task of people who are just starting to rise in the middle passage of life so difficult. As we mentioned in Chapter 5, the question faced by adults in the middle passage is "generativity or stagnation?" If you have not individuated and become your own person, then it is hard, if not impossible, for you to become generative, for you to find a new path for yourself in work, family life, or the community. The failure of family members to rise in their 20s and 30s leads to their 40s or 50s looking like the island of the Lotus-Eaters. The failure of individuation leads directly to stagnation. Our recommendations on the subjects of ownership, leadership, self-advocacy, and parenting are meant to help jump start the individuation process that may have stalled at an earlier point in life. For if individuation does not happen by or within the middle passage, then it is almost certain that you will move in the last stage of life to despair rather than integrity.

It is this failure that leads most often to the horror stories that haunt families in the land of wealth. The failure is not financial or legal. It is not a problem of asset allocation or tax strategies. It is a problem of human development, which makes it all the more complicated, but also all the more accessible. You do not have to be an expert to solve this problem. Indeed, it helps if you approach it with a beginner's mind. The solution is accessible to us all.

Searching for Elders

The work of rising is in your hands. But that does not mean that you need to face it alone. This is difficult work. As we saw when considering the island of the Lotus-Eaters, we can all use whatever help we can find.

Traditionally, human societies have ensured that certain members of the family or tribe be tasked with the special work of helping the rising generation grow and flourish. One of the strangest features of contemporary life is that we are so often expected to move through the stages of life and development on our own. Seeking help is seen as something that one does only if there is a supposed problem or hang-up. For all the great resources that families with wealth often have, it is very rare for a family to have identified people who can help members of the rising generation rise.

But individuation is not an individual task. Historically, the work of helping members of the tribe or family individuate has fallen to two types of adults: elders and mentors. In the remainder of the Conclusion, we will say a bit about each of these types. Our goal is not to provide a guide to mentors or elders but rather to offer you, members of the rising generation, some guidance in seeking out the help and counsel of these two types of people.

First, elders: Elders are not necessarily olders. They can be of varying age and experience in life. They do not have to be members of your family. A family friend can be an elder. So can a trusted adviser. The key, as we discuss in *The Cycle of the Gift*,[1] is to recognize that elders have four main roles:

1. To tell the family's stories.
2. To remind the family leaders to follow the family's agreed-upon rules.
3. To effectively mediate internal family disputes.
4. To conduct the family's rituals.

In this context, we are most concerned with the fourth of those tasks, the conduct of family rituals. Rituals do not have to involve candles and bells or intonations in dead languages. These are most often the trappings of ceremonies, which are themselves only part of a ritual. Most basically, a ritual is a journey, a passage, from one part of life to another. It involves three main elements: a break with the past, the creation of a separate space away from present-day concerns, and then a reintegration of what you have learned in that separate space back into your day-to-day life. The reintegration is the part that most often involves ceremony.

For example, when we serve as elders to families whom we know well, one of the most common rituals we conduct is the coming of age of a trust beneficiary. Often, families pass over this event with silence and secrecy. Sometimes it takes place in a pro forma manner in an attorney's office. But it can be a crucial passage in your life, as a member of the rising generation. When we conduct this ritual, we invite the upcoming beneficiary to spend a day at a neutral, peaceful location. We do not jump right into the details of the trust or legal responsibilities. Instead, we lead the beneficiary in a process of reflecting on his or her dreams, strengths, weaknesses, and goals. We probe the question of how this trust can enhance the beneficiary's life and increase his or her human capital. Only when this work is under way do we introduce the trustee or the trustee's representatives into the space we have created. The trustee's role in this ritual is to listen and to learn rather than to speak or to dictate. The goal is to create a shared understanding: that the trustee's role is to enhance the life of the beneficiary within the spirit of the legal document. This shared understanding is the true trust. With this foundation, we bring the new beneficiary and trustee back to a meeting with the family leaders, where they can share what they have learned and affirm, in a larger, more public setting, the trust they have established. This ritual lays the ground for the beneficiary's future education in the details of the trust or the allocation of its funds. It makes sure that the trust relationship will serve the family's human capital and not the other way around. It gives the beneficiary a voice.[2]

Coming of age as a trust beneficiary is only one example of a ritual. You may have many others in your life as a member of the rising generation. These may include graduating, getting married, attending your first family meeting, becoming part of your family's philanthropy, joining a family operating company board, being invited onto a family council, and eventually inviting your own children into some or all of these roles. Whatever the passage, seek out elders who can make sure you make the most of these rituals, for yourself and your family.

One more word on this point: when performing that search, remember that a true elder is not an expert. He or she may know much but is always seeking to learn more. The great English poet Alfred Tennyson captured this spirit when he imagined Odysseus as an old man in his poem "Ulysses." As Odysseus says there, "Old age hath yet its honor and its toil." And he concludes about himself and his companions, we are men who set out "to strive, to seek, to find, and not to yield." Homer predicted something similar for his Odysseus. In the underworld, Odysseus learns from the dead prophet Tiresias that, once he has returned home to Ithaca and defeated the suitors, he is to leave again, travel inland with only an oar, and not stop until he comes to a land where people have never seen the sea. His life is one of wandering and learning. So, too, for true elders.

Returning to Mentor

The other figure that can help you in the process of individuation and rising we have met already: Mentor. As you may recall, at the beginning of *The Odyssey,* Athena, the goddess of wisdom, encourages Telemachus to seek for news of his father. She does so by appearing to him in the guise of Mentor, an old family friend.

Most mentors today focus their efforts on a particular task or process of adjustment. A mentor may help you at school or at a new job or at various times in your career. But as Athena's example suggests, a true mentor does more than help you *adjust*. Athena helped Telemachus *evolve* from a boy to a man. A true mentor focuses intently on the process of individuation. It is a large calling.

A true mentor is, then, rare. What are a mentor's characteristics? Athena displays them well. First, a mentor is experienced. Most often, this experience accompanies old age, but it may be won earlier in life. Second, a mentor is trusted. Athena-Mentor is an old family friend. It takes time and familiarity for someone to become a mentor. Third, as we mentioned, a mentor does not focus just on one task or adjustment. Here is where a mentor differs from an elder. An elder works for the benefit of the whole family by helping a member move through a particular passage or transition. Compared to the mentor, the elder's work is both broader (for the good of the whole family versus strictly for the good of the mentee) and narrower (focused on a passage *in* your life rather than the evolution *of* your life). Finally, Athena's disguise reveals a very important aspect of the true mentor: being a mentor takes some wit or even guile. Authenticity is all well and good. But a mentee may not always be ready for the truth. A mentor must know how much to reveal and when. This last point means that you may meet a mentor—or perhaps have already met a mentor—and not quite know it at the time.

Like Odysseus's family, families with financial wealth today have many servants, helpers, and advisers around them at any one time. Because of their familiarity and trust, some of these advisers may be in a promising position to serve as mentors. But the sad reality is that most advisers operate within the gravitational pull of the black hole. They follow the direction of the founder or the founding dream. After all, the founder has or had a sense of purpose, growth, and vision. He or she most likely created, with advisers' help, the structures that govern the family's life. He or she laid out a path that future advisers could follow. Not unimportantly, the founders or their representatives likely hold the family's purse strings. If nothing else, the financial version of the Golden Rule—that he or she with the gold rules—likely ensures that most advisers will live within the gravity of the black hole and so serve its centripetal force. The same goes for many of the institutions (banks, trust companies, and the like) that have been specifically adapted to serve and execute upon the vision of such dreams (see Figure C.1).

Figure C.1   Advisers Inside and Outside the Boundary

This observation is not meant to blame these loyal professionals and their institutions. The very dictates of their professions incline them to serve the most readily apparent—and paying—clients' wishes. Still, it does help explain why at least 95 percent of you, the rising generation, leave your parents' advisers once you have the power to do so.[3]

They key, then, is for you to find, among the advisers or others in your life, those few or even that one who is able to stand apart from the prestige of expertise and the power of the black hole and become a true mentor. It is not a relationship that can be forced or demanded. After all, Athena, the original mentor, was a goddess. She came and went as she wished. Perhaps the best thing that you can do is to open your heart to the possibility of mentorship. In our experience, when the heart is ready, the mentor appears.

Flying Away

At the very end of *The Odyssey*, Athena once more helps her friends by pacifying the volatile situation at Ithaca. She maintains the form of Mentor, but we can easily imagine that, once her work is done, she will turn into a seagull or a shaft of light and dart away. No doubt she will continue to keep an eye on Odysseus, Telemachus, and Penelope.

Authors do not exactly have these divine abilities. Perhaps these pages will incline some of you to deepen the conversation with us personally. Perhaps for others this will be our single meeting. One of the demands of authorship is to be willing to let your work into the world without knowing what effects it will have.

Nonetheless, we are clear on one point: If this book helps even one reader awaken to the work of individuation, avoid the waking sleep of the island of the Lotus-Eaters, develop a true sense of work *and* leisure, build authentic relationships, feel greater self-confidence, find your voice and so break the otherwise deafening silence and truly rise—then we will feel that our efforts were well worth it.

At this point, then, we would recommend something that has served readers of Homer's *Odyssey* very well over the years. Even though this book is hardly to be compared with that epic, now that you have seen where the journey leads, start again from the beginning and read it once more with experienced eyes. Let the questions and the examples sink in. Then begin the most important chapter: your own journey.

Questions for Reflection

Which of the chapters that you have read speaks most to the situation and challenges you are facing now in your life? Who is someone with whom you could have an authentic conversation about what you have learned from your reading and reflection?

Notes

1. *The Cycle of the Gift: Family Wealth and Wisdom* (New York: Bloomberg, 2013), 82–83.

2. For readers who want to delve more deeply into best practices for the relationship between beneficiaries and trustees, we recommend our colleagues Hartley Goldstone and Kathy Wiseman's *Trustworthy: New Angles on Trusts from Beneficiaries and Trustees* (Denver, CO: Navigating the Trustscape, LLC, 2012).

3. Recall Michael Sisk, "How to Keep the Kids," *Barron's* (June 4, 2011), S20–S21; and Diane Doolin, Vic Preisser, and Roy Williams, "Engaging and Retaining Families," *Investments & Wealth Monitor* (September/October 2011), 10–16.

Appendix

Questions for Reflection from the End of the Chapters

From the Introduction

Think about the next six months or year of your life. What is an important choice that lies ahead of you in this space of time? Keep this choice in mind as you read the following chapters, remembering that you *do* have a choice.

From Chapter 1

Where do you stand in relation to the black hole? Who stands for you and your freedom from its gravity?

From Chapter 2

When have you had an experience of self-efficacy? What was it like?

From Chapter 3

What is an example of a belief you hold about yourself, others, or the world that gives you strength?

From Chapter 4

Pick one example each in your life of (1) true work, (2) a positive relationship, and (3) authentic communication. What makes each example distinctive?

From Chapter 5

Pick 1 of the 12 questions listed on pages 103–104 and write out your thoughts in response to it. Let it sit for a day and then revisit what you wrote. Has your response changed at all? Over the next few months, try doing the same each week for the other 11 questions.

From the Conclusion

Which of the chapters that you have read speaks most to the situation and challenges you are facing now in your life? Who is someone with whom you could have an authentic conversation about what you have learned from your reading and reflection?

Additional Tools

Our web site, www.wisecounselresearch.com, contains numerous additional readings, presentations, and handouts that can expand your understanding of the ideas discussed in this book and *The Cycle of the Gift,* as well as help you apply those ideas to your life.

We also maintain a substantial online bibliography of fictional works related to wealth as well as nonfiction readings in such areas as the history of wealth, psychology and wealth, and wealth counseling. You can find there a one-page list of Introductory Readings, which makes a great place to continue your education in this field.

Possible Educational Pathways

On many occasions, family members or their advisers have asked us if we have examples of curricula or educational materials that they can use in their family meetings or workshops. As valuable as such tools can be, there are risks in offering them. Every individual and every family is different. The art of education is to adapt general lessons to your particular situation, which is impossible to do in the appendix to a book or a model curriculum.

But the biggest risk, in this case, is that such models can too easily become expressions of the black hole that we talk about in Chapter 1. Rather than responding to the true needs and desires of you, members of the rising generation, such plans often respond to the desires and hopes of the wealth creators or the advisers who serve within their orbit. We do not want to do anything that makes it harder for you to rise.

In what follows, then, we offer three pathways. The first is for you as an individual. The second is an outline of possible workshops. And the third is the outline of a possible family meeting or set of meetings. We leave it to you to decide which path makes the most sense for you at this point in your life.

For the Individual Journey

Our primary recommendation for you, our readers, and for your advisers or parents, is that you take this book, read it yourself, reflect upon it, and continue your journey, wherever that leads. Some of you may want to make this journey alone and under your own sails. Others may seek out friends, mentors, and family members with whom to discuss these ideas and your experiences. Either path is fine. To your parents and advisers we would reiterate a message that we gave in Chapter 5: sometimes the best thing you can do for members of the rising generation is to give them space.

For Possible Workshops

Again, some of you may want to discuss the ideas in this book with other members of the rising generation who are, so to speak, in your shoes. Doing so can be a powerful aid to your own reflections and action. To make such discussion possible, we have for many years convened Wise Counsel Research Seminars, composed of members of the rising generation. While each of these gatherings has its own feel, based on the personalities of the people in the room, here is a brief description of what such workshops could look like.

We begin each new workshop by encouraging participants to share who they are and what interests brought them to the seminar. We then normalize the experience of being a member of the rising generation within a family with wealth by discussing the characteristics of that experience. Here, we draw from the material in Chapter 1 (about the power that financial wealth can have in young people's lives) and Chapter 2 (about the features of the rising generation and characteristic of Millennials in particular). Participants often find it helpful (and amusing) to locate themselves with respect to the caricatures from Chapter 1.

The core of the initial workshop is an exercise in self-reflection, aimed at beginning to think through the question, "What are my dreams?" Some of the questions we may discuss include:

- What stage of life am I in now?
- In what activities do I feel most alive?
- Do I feel that I have found a calling?

- What are my strengths?
- What do I believe about myself? About the world?
- Do my beliefs help me or hold me back?
- What does becoming my own individual look like to me?

Discussing these questions leads naturally to the last part of the workshop: identifying what areas each of you want to learn more about and how that learning will take place. For example, sometimes members of a workshop will want to expand their knowledge of investing; sometimes trustee-beneficiary mechanics are a focus; other times a group will want to go more deeply into career planning, managing relationships, or communicating with family members. Based on these decisions, we may offer follow-up workshops on such topics as "How Do I Learn Best?"; "How Do I Discover Vocation?"; "How Do I Develop Relationships of Fiscal Inequality?"; and "How Do I Learn to have Difficult Conversations?"

One point is crucial in considering whether to attend a workshop of this sort: is it your choice or someone else's? Does the workshop aim to foster your dreams, or is it another expression of the black hole? The practical consideration of who pays for your attendance is important. Many times, parents or trustees will pay for similar workshops, and as a result they explicitly or implicitly call the piper's tune. If you decide to pursue your education in this direction, you may want to consider paying some or all of the cost yourself, or at least being the one to initiate the conversation with your trustee about covering the costs. By putting your own skin in the game, you increase the probability that you will not, even unconsciously, be living someone else's dream rather than your own.

For a Possible Family Gathering

In some cases, you may want to pursue the topics in this book with your family, in a thoughtful setting such as a family meeting.

To do so is demanding work—but it can also be deeply rewarding. We have led gatherings for dozens of families, and the experience can be transformative.

For a family workshop focused on meeting the needs of you, members of the rising generation, we offer here the sketch of three sessions. Each session will likely take at least two hours to complete. While all three could theoretically be covered in one day, you would probably wear out most of your family members—if not yourself—in trying to do so. We would recommend spreading the three sessions over three meetings or, at most, covering Sessions One and Two in one day and Session Three the next (such as at a weekend gathering).

When we lead family meetings, we always use two facilitators. Doing so helps us manage the process and make sure that everyone's voice is heard. Because this set of sessions embodies something of a ritual—part of coming of age—you may also want to consider having an elder of the family preside over its beginning and end. (See the Conclusion for more on the meaning of elders.) This is certainly not a requirement, but it can add depth to the experience.

Again, this model is merely a general outline. Your family and your needs are different from others'. The key to a successful family meeting is to make sure you prepare by understanding the goals and aspirations of the participants and allow them to be heard—all while never losing sight of your own goals and dreams. Otherwise, a family meeting becomes just another extension of the black hole.

Session One: Knowing Ourselves

In this first session, we set the stage for the family by speaking about what the focus of the course is—human capital development, what human capital means, and why human capital is so important to success or failure.

To make this point about human capital "real" for participants, in the next part of the session each family member shares a story about him- or herself that captures something of his or her dreams or values. These stories may be from the far past or from the present. Besides connecting with each other, the point of the exercise is to focus participants on human capital as the family's true wealth and on stories as the medium through which that wealth is preserved and transmitted.

At this stage, we often separate the family into two parts: givers and recipients (which usually equates to parents and adult children). Each group takes up an exercise in self-understanding. We ask the givers to reflect on and discuss such questions as

- What stage of life am I in now?
- What is my true wealth?
- What are my dreams?
- Have I shared my dreams with the intended recipients of my gifts?
- How can I help members of the rising generation truly rise?

We ask you, members of the rising generation, to reflect on and discuss such questions as these:

- What stage of life am I in now?
- What are my dreams?
- In what activities do I feel most alive?
- What are my strengths?
- What do I believe about myself? About the world?
- Do my beliefs help me or hold me back?
- What does becoming my own individual look like to me?

After enough time for full reflection and discussion, we bring the groups back together. We conclude this first session by asking you, members of the rising generation, to share, in summary form, what you learned about yourselves in your reflections. This is a chance to talk about your dreams. In response, we ask that the givers talk about what they came to in their reflections, especially in regard to the question, "How can I help members of the rising generation truly rise?"

Supporting Materials for Session One

The Voice of the Rising Generation, Preface
Family Wealth, Part One, "My Philosophy"
The Cycle of the Gift, Chapter 3, "Becoming a Wise Giver"
The Voice of the Rising Generation, Chapter 3, "Self-Knowledge"
"Developmental Life Transitions" (handout on web site)

Session Two: Resilience

We begin the second session by asking for reflections, thoughts, questions, or concerns that have arisen from the first. Sometimes these reflections lead to a full discussion of their own, especially on the subject of your dreams and the ways that the older generation can help further those dreams.

We move into the rest of Session Two by reviewing the major challenges to the development of the rising generation within a family with wealth: gifts that act like meteors and the founding dream that can become a black hole. These images are powerful ones, and they often provoke a reaction. Some questions that can help guide that reaction include, "What's in your meteor?" and "Are you living within the gravity of a black hole?" You may also find it helpful and amusing to talk about the caricatures from Chapter 1 and locate yourselves (or your parents) with respect to these various caricatures.

The focus for the rest of the session is on supporting your resilience, as members of the rising generation. To start, we ask the older participants to interview you, the members of the rising generation. The starting point for each interview is the question,

"How can I invest in your dreams?" The investment we have in mind here is of the giver's human, intellectual, social, or spiritual capital for the good of the recipient; the focus is not financial. The goal of the interviewer(s) is to listen and to speak only to draw out further responses. At the end of the exercise the group reassembles and the interviewers report out a summary of what they learned about each interviewee.

You may then find it helpful, as many families do, to have a group discussion of two key areas for building resilience: work and relationships. The points captured in Chapter 4 can help structure these discussions. The first step of the conversation is to explore what to you and your parents are the characteristics of meaningful work and authentic relationships. The next step is to discuss your actual work experiences and relationships with a view to these characteristics. The overall goal is to build understanding and empathy among your family members, which in turn will support your resilience in work and relationships.

Supporting Materials for Session Two

The Cycle of the Gift, Chapter 4, "Receiving Wisely"
The Voice of the Rising Generation, Chapter 1, "Setting Sail"
The Voice of the Rising Generation, Chapter 4, "Facing the Waves"

Session Three: Action

The goal of this session is to integrate the learning from Sessions One and Two into a plan for taking action following the meetings.

Again, we begin by reviewing what you covered in Sessions One and Two and asking for your thoughts or questions.

The plan for the rest of the session depends on the areas of possible action open to your family. Some of those areas include parenting minors, overseeing a family business enterprise, engaging in family philanthropy, navigating grantor-trustee-beneficiary relationships, and managing family financial wealth. In preparation, we always make sure that we know before the session which of these domains are applicable to the family and have a plan for reviewing the landscape of each applicable domain. Our goal is not to review each domain as experts (e.g., discussing how each trust works or what the succession plan for the business is) but rather to help you and the rest of your family think through such questions as:

- Which of these domains is doing well and should continue as is?
- In which of these domains do we feel we could be doing more to increase our human capital, especially the human capital of the rising generation?
- What are the steps we can take to do that?

Our hope is that this review of the family landscape allows each of you, members of the rising generation, to create an individual development plan for further learning, experiences, or growth opportunities. Sometimes we also recommend additional self-understanding exercises—which can help you learn more about how you learn. This is also a place where we often ask members of the rising generation to talk about whether you have mentors who can help you in this process of learning about yourself and pursuing your dreams.

To close the meeting, we offer you, members of the rising generation, a chance to summarize what you have learned in the three sessions and the steps you plan to take on the basis of that learning. These steps may involve further education in such areas as investments, trusts, management of the family business, and financial or estate planning. They may include personal exploration and growth. Whatever your individual path, the role of the older family members in this closing ceremony is to listen and affirm.

Supporting Materials for Session Three

The Voice of the Rising Generation, Chapter 5, "The Middle Passage"

The Voice of the Rising Generation, Conclusion

Family: the Compact among Generations, Chapter 19, "Educational Assessment Tools"

About the Authors

James E. Hughes, Jr., Esq

Jay, a resident of Aspen, Colorado, a retired attorney, is the author of *Family Wealth: Keeping It in the Family*, and of *Family—The Compact Among Generations,* and numerous articles on family governance and wealth preservation as well as a series of Reflections, which can be found on the Articles section of his web site www.jamesehughes.com. He was the founder of a law partnership in New York City and has spoken frequently at numerous international and domestic symposia on the avoidance of the shirtsleeves to shirtsleeves proverb and the growth of families' human, intellectual, social, and spiritual capital as supported by their financial capital toward their families' flourishing. He is a member of various philanthropic boards and a member of the editorial boards of various professional journals. He is a graduate of the Far Brook School, which teaches through the arts; the

Pingry School; Princeton University; and the Columbia School of Law.

Dr. Susan E. Massenzio

Susan is a psychologist and president of Wise Counsel Research Associates, a think-tank and consultancy.

Susan has many years' experience consulting to senior executives, leadership teams of Fortune 100 companies, and heads of family businesses. She helps firms develop high potential executives, plan leadership succession, and integrate key leaders into new roles. She helps family leaders make a positive impact through enhanced communication, decision making, cultivation of the next generation, and philanthropy.

Susan served for many years as the senior psychologist for John Hancock Financial Services, a senior vice president at Wells Fargo Family Wealth, and professor and program director at Northeastern University.

Susan is a member of the Collaboration for Family Flourishing. She holds a PhD in psychology from Northwestern University and a BA in sociology and education from Simmons College.

In addition to her writing and speaking, Susan consults with select executives and heads of family enterprises around leadership, organizational development, and individual and family flourishing. If you would like to discuss an initial consultation, please contact Susan at susan@wisecounselresearch.com.

Dr. Keith Whitaker

Keith is an educator and founding associate with Wise Counsel Research Associates, a think-tank and consultancy. His early introduction to the tradition of liberal education excited his fascination with the cycle of the gift.

Keith has many years' experience consulting with advisers to and leaders of enterprising families. He helps families plan succession, develop next-generation talent, and communicate around estate planning. With a background in education and philanthropy, he enables family leaders to better understand their values and goals as well as to have a positive impact on the world around them.

Keith served as a managing director at Wells Fargo, where he founded the innovative Family Dynamics Practice. He has also served as a researcher at the Boston College Center on Wealth and Philanthropy, a private trustee, a director of a private foundation, and a philosophy professor at Boston College.

Keith's writings and commentary have appeared in *The Wall Street Journal*, *The New York Times*, the *Financial Times*, and *Philanthropy Magazine*. His *Wealth and the Will of God* (co-authored with Dr. Paul Schervish) appeared in 2010 from Indiana University Press.

Keith is a member of the Boston Estate Planning Council and a founding member of the Collaboration for Family Flourishing. He holds a PhD in Social Thought from the University of Chicago and a BA and MA in classics and philosophy from Boston University.

Keith speaks regularly about the themes of *The Cycle of the Gift* with families, membership organizations, and trade groups. If you would like to discuss a speaking engagement, please contact Keith at keith@wisecounselresearch.com.

Index